D0916013

Women
Street
Hustlers

Women Street Hustlers

Who They Are and How They Survive

Barbara A. Rockell

American Psychological Association • Washington, DC

Published by
American Psychological Association
750 First Street, NE
Washington, DC 20002
www.apa.org

To order
APA Order Department
P.O. Box 92984
Washington, DC 20090-2984
Tel: (800) 374-2721; Direct: (202) 336-5510
Fax: (202) 336-5502; TDD/TTY: (202) 336-6123
Online: www.apa.org/books/
E-mail: order@apa.org

In the U.K., Europe, Africa, and the Middle East, copies may be ordered from
American Psychological Association
3 Henrietta Street
Covent Garden, London
WC2E 8LU England

Typeset in Minion by Circle Graphics, Inc., Columbia, MD

Printer: Maple-Vail Manufacturing Group, Binghamton, NY
Cover Designer: Mercury Publishing Services, Rockville, MD
Technical/Production Editor: Devon Bourexis

The opinions and statements published are the responsibility of the author, and such opinions and statements do not necessarily represent the policies of the American Psychological Association.

Library of Congress Cataloging-in-Publication Data

Rockell, Barbara A.
  Women street hustlers : who they are and how they survive / Barbara A. Rockell.
    p. cm.
  Includes bibliographical references and index.
  ISBN-13: 978-1-4338-0333-8
  ISBN-10: 1-4338-0333-X
  1. Female offenders—New York (State)—Case studies. 2. Women prisoners—New York (State)—Case studies. I. American Psychological Association. II. Title.

  HV6046.R55 2008
  364.3'7409747—dc22
                              2007038986

British Library Cataloguing-in-Publication Data
A CIP record is available from the British Library.

Printed in the United States of America
First Edition

In loving memory and honor of my parents,
Thomas K. and Annette M. Rockell,
and with much appreciation and gratitude to
Hans Toch

Contents

Preface

The streets are my living room, bedroom, and front porch.
The bodegas—they're my kitchen and refrigerator, and the laundromat,
bus station, or off-track betting parlor—that's my bathroom.

—Judy

I have been told that if you ask anyone who works in a jail, be they men or women, whether they would rather supervise male or female inmates, their answer uniformly and without hesitation would be males.[1] Just as unvaried and quickly given would be the reasons for this preference, all of which reflect widely disputed yet lasting stereotypes about gender. According to these thoughts and images, women, and especially female inmates living in a world without men, appear as caricatures of their supposed worst tendencies, traits, and characteristics. They are said to be obstinate and demanding, never taking no for an answer and always wanting to know why something is forbidden or taken away from them; they are described as overly emotional and hormonally imbalanced, particularly when trying to live together in groups, where each tries to exceed the other in terms of drama-laden accounts or outbursts; they are called catty, always getting into each other's business and gossiping incessantly; and, most important,

---

[1] Although other scholars have noted the existence of this male preference among correctional officers (e.g., Pollock, 1986), the sources for the remarks noted throughout this preface are jail deputies themselves, primarily at the Monroe County Correctional Facility, the site of this study.

they are thought to be bitchy with each other and staff, never reluctant to fight, even if weaponless, and always noisy and nasty when doing so.

I, of course, do not subscribe to any of these thoughts about women or female inmates in particular, and what follows is not a discourse about jails, nor is it an examination of inmate behavior in them. Instead, the stories retold in this book are about the women who regularly go to jail, especially the typical large American jail: chronic low-level female offenders who are both of the street and on it, committing a wide variety of hustles for just as many reasons to support their forlorn existence at the margins of society.

I decided to preface this book with remarks about jails because there is a certain symmetry between these local institutions and the women they house. Both, for instance, are relatively invisible, or at least unknown, to scholars and the public at large. Our fascination, it seems, is with prisons and the felons they hold—after all, we often hear, "What life is there to study in jails—institutions where individuals typically serve a year or less—what culture or behaviors of interest could there possibly be?" The public's lack of interest is even more pronounced: In fact, it is likely that most citizens in any given jurisdiction have no idea where their local jail is and probably never will until they, a family member, or a friend becomes incarcerated in it.

Just as invisible as the structures themselves are the women who populate this nation's jails. In fact, a common expression heard throughout my study was that "jails are built and run by men to house men—we [women] are just an afterthought or inconvenience . . . herded into whatever space is left after the men get theirs." This perceived or felt invisibility is, of course, arguable; what is not, however, is the reaction many jail officials have to the burdens presented by female inmates, which, indeed, may explain their previously described negative attributions. It is, for instance, commonly known that jail administrators often look upon women detainees and commitments as if they were one classification (i.e., female), taking up scarce, and therefore valuable, cell space and demanding attention for a host of medical, emotional, or mental health problems that they as administrators are typically unequipped to handle. Moreover, the very introduction of women into what is a predominantly male dominion is usually dreaded in and of itself, presenting, as it does, the unlikely but feared opportunity for sexual relationships among inmates and the more likely and just as feared allegations of sexual harassment against those who supervise them.

There is yet another commonality between jails and the women they hold, one that is shared with their local male counterparts, and that is the stigma or status conferred by poverty. The marks of this privation are overwhelming. Both are untended and physically worn by years of neglect and violence at the margins of society, and more important, both are rarely thought to be deserving of public notice, aid, or assistance to improve or rise above their impoverished state. One cannot help but wonder if it is the nature of the people in jail that limits our interest in and attention to these facilities. They are, after all, Irwin's (1975) "rabble" and Goldfarb's (1975) "ghetto," the marginalized of society who exist off its vices and survive on the streets that most of us will not travel. They are not the serial murderers portrayed in our media, and they are not the "monsters" we try to understand and, perhaps, correct in penitentiaries that are supposedly constructed for this purpose. They, and especially the women among them, are the "disreputables," the deviant sex and dope fiends who haunt our streets and end up in what is typically the most blighted of all public institutions: the jail.

The remaining similarity between jails and their female inmates—and that which more than anything prompted this study—is the fact that both are surrounded by misinformation, misunderstanding, and mistaken assumptions. Just as jails are not synonymous with prisons or minimum security institutions (a couple of common misconceptions), chronic low-level female offenders, the reader will see, are not necessarily sad, hapless creatures who steal or hook simply to feed their chronic addictions because they are helpless and unable to do anything else.

It was Eleanor Miller's (1986) *Street Women* that piqued my scholarly interest in these women, and it was with the intent to pick up where she left off that I began this study. In doing so, I particularly wanted to explore how the markedly changed economic environment of inner cities had affected the social relations and processes that Miller implicated in her recruitment routes of women to low-level crime. Considered just as relevant were (a) the far more virulent drug scene (crack had not yet appeared on the streets of Miller's Milwaukee), (b) the punitive shift in crime control policies,

(c) the skewed gender ratio in the inner city and the record level incarceration of so many young minority males, and (d) the differing gender identity constructions. I thought all of these social and economic occurrences were powerful enough to suggest a renewed look at street women.

There are a few differences between this book and that of E. Miller (1986). First, I have elected not to use the term *street women*, as Miller did, in reference to the women in this study. Although certainly descriptive of their criminality, lives, and location, the expression also carries with it connotations (i.e., that these women are solely streetwalkers) that are both deceptive and untrue. I, instead, choose to refer to them as E. Miller subsequently did (Romensko & Miller, 1989), as *street hustlers*, for hustling is what they do to survive, whether it be for property to boost (i.e., sell), sex to exchange for money, or drugs to sell or buy.

I also prefer the expression *street hustler* for these women because it captures so nicely and precisely their opportunistic, dog-eat-dog worldview and take on life. Unlike much of what has been written about female offenders that stresses their woeful childhoods, deficient educations, lacking job skills, and painful relationships, the stories recounted here tell of their hustling abilities—their strengths, resources, and wits that enable them to survive, albeit at the margins of society. As stated earlier, these are not hapless women, defined solely by their presence on the street; in fact, the reader will learn that there is much about them that demonstrates a unique set of street smarts encompassing not only survival skills but also a sharp insight—an acumen, if you will—into both people and their business with them.

My inquiry also was framed very differently than E. Miller's (1986) and included perspectives, particularly those of microsociology (Scheff, 1990) and social psychology (Bandura, 1997; Fleisher, 1995; Goffman, 1959; Lofland, 1969; Maruna, 2001; McGuire, 2004; Matza, 1969; Samenow, 2004; Terry, 2003), that hers did not. These bodies of literature were consulted because of my interest in understanding what the women themselves thought about their lives and their crimes. My research, thus, extended beyond the etiological to examine the women close-up for their perceptions and subjective realities of the lives they led, the streets they frequented, and the hustles they practiced.

Finally, unlike E. Miller (1986), I was interested in female misdemeanants and not felons, and because women street hustlers spend good portions of their lives alternating time between jail and the street, I elected not to do field research and, instead, went to a large urban jail, specifically a county correctional facility, to find my sample. The use of the jail also figured into my research plan, as I was interested in the role it played in the women's lives, as they perceived it, as well as the effects it had, both material and nonmaterial, on sustaining, or perhaps maintaining, their marginal street existence.

I was very privileged and honored to work with Hans Toch on this endeavor. Not only is Dr. Toch an incredible teacher, with his patient mentoring, shared insights, and strong editorial skills, all of which were invaluable to this new student, he is also a brilliant scholar of people, who wholly supported and encouraged my interest to just listen. I will never forget our daily talks (via e-mail) and Dr. Toch's unbelievable commitment and efforts over the past few years to help make my return to academia a successful one.

I also give a special thanks to the current and former Monroe County Sheriffs, Patrick M. O'Flynn and Andrew P. Meloni, for the access and support they provided. And, finally, there are 60 women whom I wish I could name and thank individually for their participation in this study. Their willingness to sit with me in a "corridor cell"[2] for hours and tell their story "for the book" will always be remembered and appreciated.

---

[2] In the jail where this research took place, the expression *corridor cell* refers to cells used for isolation or disciplinary purposes.

Women
Street
Hustlers

Introduction: Understanding the Lives of Women Street Hustlers

They speak a language of their own, these women I am talking to in the jail, a language of words that I have never heard spoken, especially in the context in which they are said. There is one word in particular, the word *lick,* that everyone seems to use, be they a booster,[1] a prostitute, or a self-proclaimed addict. After much thought about how and when it was said, I think I have finally figured out what the word means and am amused at the simplicity of this message-laden expression.[2] When a woman tells me that her daily criminal activity involves "catching a good lick," she is speaking of hustling someone out of something, getting up on someone, or "licking" that person at something.

For most of these women it seems that the monetary outcome of this lick goes to the dealer who supplies their first drugs of the morning, their wake-up call to "stay off dope sick" or "stay off E." Most, in fact, seem to have established a sort of credit score with a supplier who is in close proximity and usually available to front them money for that crucial first hit of the day. I remember asking the rather uninformed question, "Why don't you just keep a bit from the night before?" and hearing the incredulous response, "Because there never is any bit and there never would be—I'd smoke it." I also recall the first time I heard the expression "off E" and asked

---

[1] A *booster* is someone who shoplifts and then sells the stolen goods. The women were very familiar with this term and used it frequently.

[2] I recently accessed an online urban dictionary (http://www.urbandictionary.com) and found *lick* defined as "any instance where you come upon easy money."

naively, "Do you mean coffee?" For the women with whom I am talking, staying off E, or "off empty of drugs," is critical to avoiding what each person dreads: "dope sickness," the debilitating and gut-wrenching symptoms characteristic of withdrawal.

I learned many other words during the course of the research conducted for this book and much more from and about the women who used them. These women are known to jail staff as "regulars" or "old timers" (which, of course, refers not to chronological age but to the number of times one has been in jail). They are your common female urban street offenders, convicted of numerous low-level property, public order, and drug offenses. In criminological literature, they would be equivalent to the male chronic offenders, those 5% or 6% of offenders responsible for most crime, whom Maruna (2001) so cleverly described as "infamous" and "the obsession of criminologists," even though they are but "petty thieves, vandals, and punks" (p. 13).

Although it is true that the actual number of women in U.S. jails remains low compared with the number of men who are detained or incarcerated, this should not overshadow the fact that women have been coming to jail over the past 10 years at a rate of increase that surpasses that of men. The Bureau of Justice Statistics (2005) reported, for instance, that from 1995 to 2004 the adult female jail population experienced an average rate of increase of 7.0% annually, compared with a 4.2% annual rate of increase for men. Also, over the 12-month period ending June 30, 2004, the disparity between the rates of increase for female and male admissions was even greater, with women continuing to reflect their 10-year average with an increase in population of 6.6%, compared with men, whose numbers increased just 2.8%. More recently, the Bureau of Justice Statistics (2007) indicated that like jail growth nationally, the rate of increase for female inmates has slowed. In spite of this slowed growth, however, the rate of increase among adult female inmates still remains higher than that among men. Thus, between July 1, 2005, and June 30, 2006, "the number of adult females in local jails grew at a faster rate (4.9%) than the number of adult males (2.2%)" (p. 5). Data also show that "from 2000 to 2006, the number of adult females in local jails increased by 40% compared to 22% for adult males" (p. 5). Although I must again stress that actual numbers of women in jail pale in comparison to the number of men, these rates of increase are a cause of some concern, especially for facilities that are often generally ill equipped and ill staffed to deal with women.

Despite the commonality or daily presence of chronic low-level female offenders in most urban jails, we actually know relatively little about these women. In fact, the majority of information that we have on them is descriptive, at best, and derived primarily from national data collection efforts and individual studies driven by public health concerns. These data tell us much about the "what for" and "who" of women confined in jail, and we can thus speak with some confidence about the offenses for which women are being detained or incarcerated, and we can describe who they are in terms of certain background, social, economic, and health-related issues. We know fairly little, however, about the whole person, how she accounts for lifestyle choices she has made and not made and how she portrays her activities, conventional and otherwise, to survive.

In fact, in much of the literature, the reasons and motivations behind what a woman does with respect to criminality remain unexplored and mired in assumptions about forces that drive her to crime, especially those related to gender, which even if not explicitly stated, often continue to provide the backdrop for everything she does as a person or offender (see J. Miller, 2001). She is, in other words, a woman first, with her gendered background typically dictating her gendered criminality. Therefore, gender—or what it means to grow up and live as one gender or another, in this case, the female gender—seems to be all-controlling in explaining both women's initial criminal involvement and their subsequent offending behavior. Thus, her path to criminality is usually one in which oppression or victimization figures prominently, in response to which she self-medicates her pain with drugs or continues to make bad choices regarding men in her gendered quest as a woman for love and family. The drugs lead to addiction, which is typically fostered by significant others, and the addiction leads to her continued presence on the street, where criminal opportunities remain gender based or bound, and she does the only thing available to her as a woman to survive (i.e., sex work).

This overreliance on gender to explain everything also seems to limit what is assumed about the chronic woman offender's daily survival and "street life cycle" (Fleisher, 1995, p. 9). With respect to the former (i.e., daily survival), primary emphasis usually is placed on the role of men in sheltering and sustaining her in "alternative living arrangements in the inner-city crack culture" (Maher, Dunlap, Johnson, & Hamid, 1996), with far less attention given to other individual or structural resources she may have or develop (Maher, Dunlap, & Johnson, 2006; Romenesko & Miller, 1989). Similarly, her street life cycle, because of a lack of scrutiny, is merely assumed to mirror that of her male counterpart, whereby once she leaves her family of origin, time is alternated between stays in the sanctuaries of the street (i.e., missions and shelters) and those of the system (i.e., jail and prison), until age dictates otherwise (Fleisher, 1995).

Exceptions in the literature exist, of course, especially in the relatively large subfield of work that has focused on prostitution-related activity (e.g., see Fullilove & Lown, 1992; Green, Day, & Ward, 2000; Maxwell & Maxwell, 2000; Monto, 2004; Norton-Hawk, 2004; Ratner, 1993; Surratt, Inciardi, Kurtz, & Kiley, 2004; Williamson & Cluse-Tolar, 2002). However, although these studies certainly have provided much insight into the dynamics and contours of street sex work, with few exceptions (e.g., see Dalla, Xia, & Kennedy, 2003; Erickson, Butters, McGillicuddy, & Hallgren, 2000; Maher, 1992, 1997; Maher et al., 1996) they have told us little about the whole woman both on and off the street: how she survives and the arrangements she makes to live, the social connections she develops to feel and be safe, and the range of conventional and unconventional activities she might pursue to generate income.

In fact, one could argue, as I do in this book, that sex work often constitutes just one aspect of urban street women's lives and that it and they cannot be fully understood without a much broader focus that examines the individual within the context of both her offending career and the criminal opportunity structures available in her community of activity. Moreover, the usefulness or generalizability of works in this area has been hampered by the locale of the research, which typically has been the big city environment; as a result, the knowledge provided and theories generated are restricted spatially to social and economic conditions that may or may not apply in other urban settings (e.g., see Fagan, 1994; Inciardi, Lockwood, & Pottieger, 1993; Maher, 1997; Maher & Daly, 1996; Maxwell & Maxwell, 2000; Mieczkowski, 1994; Sommers, Baskin, & Fagan, 1996, 2000).

These limitations pertaining to the lack of study and theorizing about low-level women offenders are in sharp contrast to the state of research about female felons or prison-situated women. No longer invisible in the literature, these women and their life experiences have been examined within the context of differing theoretical perspectives through a variety of research methods. In comparison, the study of women in jail or of women offenders who typically commit a variety of low-level crimes and frequently see local confinement but rarely prison stays has remained mired in assumptions and themes that have only recently been challenged in the literature (e.g., see Denton & O'Malley, 2006; Maher et al., 2006). I discuss these characteristics of studies of low-level women offenders more fully in the next chapter; however, for the necessity and purpose of contextualizing the present research, I highlight them briefly here as well.

PREVALENT THEMES IN THE LITERATURE

Primary among the themes in studies examining women's entry into and involvement in low-level illicit activities is their lack of agency or their actual passivity in decision making with respect to criminality (e.g., see Daly, 1992; Denton & O'Malley, 2006; Inciardi et al., 1999; Maher, 1992, 1997; Maher & Daly, 1996). Thus, in the works cited, the women appear acted on by forces beyond their control, whether a history of relational abuse, the throes of addiction, love for a man, sexism in the criminal underworld, or a narrowing of legitimate options with each crime committed. Their offense histories, then, are presented as a mirror image of this lack of choice, and they appear driven to crime or, more typically, gendered forms of law breaking, such as prostitution and theft, with minimal agency or decision making either apparent or possible. Whether a victim of their past, drugs, men, or gender, they remain propelled into crime, with few resources and even fewer choices in what they do as offenders or how they survive as persons.

I argue here, as has been argued elsewhere, that this characterization of female offenders as being a reactive as opposed to an active agent in criminality deflects attention away from larger economic and structural conditions at the community and neighborhood levels that may have far more potency in explaining and understanding the street lives and existence of these low-level offenders (e.g., see Maher & Daly, 1996; Maher et al., 2006; Maxwell & Maxwell, 2000; Mieczkowski, 1994; Sommers et al., 1996, 2000). I further argue that because of this ignorance of context, the illicit behaviors and street-level existence of low-level women offenders often appear irrational or merely symptomatic remnants of a history of harm, when they may indeed be reflective of other needs and motivations, or perhaps even intelligible (e.g., see Denton & O'Malley, 2006).

In much of the early literature the most significant force compelling women to crime was drug use and addiction, which was typically cast as a form of self-medication to deal with the trauma of a history of abuse (e.g., see Arnold, 1990; Daly, 1992; Gilfus, 1992; Inciardi et al., 1999; Ritchie, 1996). This was especially the case with respect to explaining women's involvement in sex work and prostitution, seen as the only means of revenue available to the addicted woman for obtaining her next fix. The overwhelming power of addiction also appears implicated, however, in studies of other forms of illicit–income generating activities typically associated with women, from shoplifting and boosting to welfare and bank fraud (Denton & O'Malley, 2006, p. 203).

More recent research challenges this image of the drug-driven female criminal and what is, in effect, a singular cause-and-effect model in which drug use is an all-consuming activity that directs all aspects of a person's life, especially that pertaining to crime, which presumably is done solely to finance one's particular habit (e.g., see Denton & O'Malley, 2006; Maher et al., 2006). These recent studies, in fact, raise the possibility that there may be a great deal more variability among low-level woman offenders or street women than was previously thought and that this variability may be due to both individual-level factors, such as skill levels and motivation, as well as more structural-level considerations related to the criminal opportunities associated with place of activity or residence (e.g., see Morgan & Joe, 1997). This scholarship also stresses the importance of the temporal dimension or the need to approach the study of these offenders with attention paid to where they are at present and have been in terms of their illicit careers (e.g., see Denton & O'Malley, 2006).

The prevalence in the literature of what can only be called a *mono-thematic approach* to the study of low-level women offenders speaks to the need for the research that was conducted for this book. Its significance lies in the intent to bring the whole woman into focus, to understand not just her beginnings in crime but also what she has done over time in that life and why. Furthermore, the woman does not stand alone in this inquiry but is placed at the scene of the crime, so to speak. What she does and has done criminally is examined contextually, in other words, in terms of the people, places, and things thought to be influential in her development both as a person and as an offender. Her survival while criminally involved is likewise examined for practices and norms characteristic of particular types of offenders, as well as those common to all who frequent and exist on the street.

THE PATHS TAKEN

As stated, the intent of the research conducted for this book was to address the limitations in knowledge about chronic low-level women offenders and to do so in a way that brings the whole person into focus, using the women's own words, expressions, and thoughts to understand the who, what, where, when, how, and why of their life courses. I began with an eye to their past by getting a sense of who these women were and how they saw themselves as individuals. I did this by having the women talk about each stage of their lives from childhood and adolescence to adulthood in terms of what they thought were the most influential forces on them, be they people, events, experiences, relationships, or places. I then asked the women to talk about their involvement in crime, with an emphasis on describing the contours of this activity, its frequency, duration, specialization or diversity, and productivity within their life experiences. Finally, at the most basic, but relatively unexamined level I explored with the women how they survived while they were criminally active. In particular, I asked them about the various interpersonal and structural resources and arrangements, both legal and illegal, they had used to survive, and what that survival actually looked like and entailed. I also questioned the women about the meaning or place of jail in their lives and how it functioned to sustain, or perhaps maintain, them in their marginal street existence.

I undertook this project, of course, within the context of existing research literature. More specifically, three bodies of work directed how I shaped the initial inquiry. The first, which informed the examination of women's entry into street-level crime, has been categorized as "pathways research" (Belknap, 2007, p. 70) and is conceptualized here as demonstrative of the broader theoretical perspective of developmental criminology (e.g., see Kelley, Loeber, Keenan, & DeLamatre, 1997; Sampson & Laub, 1993; Thornberry & Krohn, 2001). The pathways approach is so named because of its emphasis on detailing and conceptualizing significant life events, as recounted by research participants, into trajectories that result in criminal involvement (Belknap, 2007).

The second body of literature that directed this study focused on women's involvement in the recent and current underground urban drug economy (specifically that pertaining to crack cocaine and heroin), either directly as players in the preparation, sale, and distribution of drugs, or indirectly as users who allegedly are criminally involved to support their addictions (Baskin & Sommers, 1998; Baskin, Sommers, & Fagan, 1993; Bourgois, 1989; Bourgois & Dunlap, 1993; Fagan, 1994; Maher, 1997; Maher & Daly, 1996; Maher et al., 1996; Mieczowski, 1994; Sommers et al., 1996; Steffensmeier, 1983; Steffensmeier & Terry, 1986). The third theoretical tradition I consulted was urban sociology or, more specifically, the subfields of urban community studies and the social networks perspective within this tradition (Anderson, 1990, 1999; Bourgois, 2003; Maher, 1996, 1997; Suttles, 1968; Wilson, 1997).

GUIDEPOSTS AND DETOURS ALONG THE WAY

At each juncture of this endeavor I found myself challenged with interpreting what I was finding within the context of the literature. Also, as I started to see themes, some of which were consistent with the works that framed my inquiry and others that were not, I realized that I would have to cast my net wider with respect to the literature and theoretical foundations for my study. This was, in fact, the only way that I could make sense out of what I was learning.

I found, for instance, that pathways research seemed far too linear and deterministic in accounting for these women's involvement in crime and that it often obscured—and in some cases, totally ignored—what the women themselves said about their backgrounds and histories. In fact, the women's subjective realities about their upbringings and the meanings they attached to them did not always match what appeared to be the objective, harsh conditions under which they had been raised. These women rarely affixed blame for their criminality on mothers or grandmothers who struggled to raise them, using whatever means they could, telling me that "They did the best that they could."[3] Also, many did not interpret their early involvement in crime, if such were the case, as anything more than a "part of growing up" or "just the way things were in the neighborhood"; one had to "act tough" or be "rude and bad," they told me, simply to survive "on the street."

I also found that for some women the continued commission of crime was not typically need or drug based, at least initially, as suggested by both pathways literature and research related to the gendered drug scene. Instead, what appeared to be operative for a number of them was the lure or lifestyle associated with crime or, as Owen (1998) so descriptively termed it, *la vida loca* (i.e., the crazy life). Others honestly seemed to express an addiction-like quality to crime and described how they felt when doing it in language similar to that so richly captured by Jack Katz (1988) in his book *Seductions of Crime*. One said, "It was better than going to the clubs," and others indicated that crime was "a high, a rush, an addiction like my drugs and scratch-offs [games of chance]."

There even were a number of women, those with high aspirations in spite of their upbringings in severe poverty, whose intense need for material objects, wealth, and the best, especially for their children, seemed to indicate some form of resistance or reaction formation to their own early status of deprivation. Then there were women with emotional and/or mental disabilities who told me that, when using crack, they not only felt normal but also in control of or superior to their old, limited selves. This sense of enhanced self-esteem and self-efficacy was further intensified by their criminal involvements and even their frequent stays

---

[3] Unless attributed to a particular author, the text in quotations and that which follows represent comments made by the women of this study.

in jail, where they seemed to define themselves as being bad rather than mad. Finally, there were women who were the most damaged by lives of repeated loss and trauma; they continued to feel these losses deeply and seemed to be expressing this with everything they did on the street and how they did it, with their quasi- or street families, if you will.

I also did not find prior research pertaining to the gendered drug scene particularly informative or helpful in interpreting what I uncovered with respect to the exercise and manifestation of gender among these women of the street. It is true that I did find confirmation for the literature that speaks to the continued existence of blocked opportunities for women in the drug world (e.g., Maher & Daly, 1996), because very few admitted to occupying managerial or higher positions in the various drug markets in their communities, and most could identify only one woman who had attained such a status, speaking her street name with awe and respect, as if she were a legend. However, what I did see and hear from the women were reflections on how gender influenced the accommodations they had made to carve out a niche in their local drug world, even if it meant restricting their sales to low weights or traveling to neighboring rural towns where they didn't have to worry about male competition and could exploit residents' ignorance about drugs and prices. There were many more instances in which these women used their gender, or assumptions about it, to make it in the criminal world, as well as that pertaining to drugs exclusively. Readers will find these and other observations in the pages that follow.

Constructions of gender also entered into the means and arrangements these women used to survive life on the streets and to feel and stay safe in that environment. Furthermore, although these women's street lives might appear to be a chaotic jungle to those on the outside, they were in fact thick with certain practices; shared understandings; norms; and community institutions that facilitated a measure of existence, although marginal at best. Just as common and normative was what one needed to see and access these practices, and that was the outlook or take on life that all of the women shared: the lick or street smarts to spot an opportunity to get up on someone or obtain something with minimal effort and by wits alone.

SOME FINAL COMMENTS

In a sense, there were several "black boxes" that I wanted to fill with this research. These theoretical interests represented three progressive time frames in the women's lives. First, I wanted to know something about the backgrounds of the women, addressing not just their interpersonal relationships and histories of victimization, as much of the literature does, but also inquiring as to the role of "broader social, economic, and cultural [worlds along with] immediate, specific, and local contexts in structuring the conditions by which [their] agency [was] enacted" (Maher, 1997, p. 1).

The second black box I wished to fill was that dealing with the women's motivations or apparent proximate reasons for committing crime. I accomplished this not only by asking each woman why she did what she did but also by inquiring about the "how" of her criminality and what these actions might imply about her motivations (Katz, 1988). The final black box was that time in each woman's life when she was out of jail and trying to eke out survival on the street: I wanted to know about her daily life, how she survived while criminally active, and what her niche was or how she fit at the margins of society.

The life stories of 60 street women or women hustlers follow. These represent the entire population of women offenders sentenced to the jail during the summer and fall of 2005 who met the following three selection criteria: (a) recidivist status or at least five prior jail sentences; (b) offense type, meaning low-level property, drug, and public order convictions; and (c) the absence of prison commitments in the woman's history.

For a few of the women in my sample, jail stays had been a regular and frequent part of their lives for more than 30 years. For considerably more, the familiar trip to and from jail had spanned at least 10 years of their adult lives, and for one woman life began in jail, when her mother delivered her as one of the first babies born at Bedford Hills Correctional Facility in Westchester County, New York. All of the women had past commitments to jail for a variety of misdemeanors, including, but not limited to, petty larcenies, prostitution, and drug-related activity. Most were mothers, some with their own children now in jail or prison, and all but two were daughters, sisters, nieces, or cousins of others who had been incarcerated or killed as a result of criminal involvement or street violence.

THE CHAPTERS AHEAD

There are two parts to this book. Part I, consisting of three chapters, essentially sets the stage for my subsequent discussion of the study's findings and implications. In chapter 2, the first chapter of this part, I critically review the current literature and research dealing with chronic low-level women offenders. As stated earlier, three bodies of literature are examined: (a) pathways research, associated with the feminist tradition of the use of life histories as a methodological tool; (b) research, primarily that which is ethnographic, that targets women's involvement in the recent and current drug scene; and (c) urban sociology, or, more specifically, the subfields of urban community studies and the social networks perspective within that tradition. In addition, I highlight motivational themes derived from urban sociology and then contextualize them within relevant social psychological and psychological literature.

In chapter 3, I introduce readers to the research conducted for this book, in what is termed the *Rochester Study*. I use this chapter to answer the most basic questions about my inquiry; accordingly, I detail the who, what, why, and how of the research, which is characterized as quasi-ethnography (Owen, 1998, p. 20). I conclude this overview by introducing three concepts related to my research interests that will frame subsequent discussions and interpretations of the study's findings. These concepts, referred to as "research outcomes," are the following: (a) hustling pathways, (b) hustling outlooks, and (c) hustling lifestyles (Fleisher, 1995).

In the final chapter of Part I, chapter 4, I discuss in detail how the research was designed and conducted. My use of life histories to construct distinct profiles of the women is explained, as are the methods I used to collect qualitative data for this purpose. The chapter concludes with a review of the analytic procedures that directed my work with and interpretation of the data.

My findings and discussion of them are presented in the four chapters of Part II. I open chapter 5 with a brief description of the physical environment and social milieu of the city where my sample lived and worked. I then introduce what I found in the data with respect to the women's six distinct pathways to the street. In chapter 6, I examine each of these groups more closely in terms of their criminality and criminal lifestyles. Profiles of who the women were and what they became as offenders also are provided. In chapter 7, the final chapter in which I discuss my findings, the street and jail survival of the women, as an aggregate, is detailed.

A thorough review and analysis of my findings are provided in chapter 8, in which I also highlight areas recommended for future research. The chapter begins with an examination of the six hustling trajectories in terms of such factors as victimization history, personal resources, and social forces. I also discuss the apparent meaning of hustling to the women in each group with respect to its place in personal narratives and its role in enhancing feelings of self-efficacy or expressing deeper psychological issues.

I then describe how each group changed over time in terms of the women's pattern of criminality. I frame this discourse by referencing certain dimensions associated with the women's offense histories, including their motivational aspects, facilitating opportunity structures, and normative practices. I conclude with an examination of the women's hustling lifestyle, both on the street and in the jail, focusing on the personal skills, community institutions, and shared understandings that facilitate at least marginal survival in each venue.

PART ONE

PURPOSE,
PLAN,
PROJECT

2

A Critical Review of the Research Literature

Caricature-like imagery has dominated criminological literature dealing with women and crime since Lombroso and Ferrero's atavistic woman offender made her first, albeit fleeting, appearance in 1893.[1] Although certainly not as extreme (and racially driven) today, dimensionless profiles continue to be seen, with two opposing characterizations paramount in the literature, both of which are shaped by thoughts about gender, its meaning, actualization, and representation, in society (Daly, 1992).

The first characterization, which is grounded in the assumption of a patriarchal society, suggests a gender script for women marked by passivity and oppression, leading to the argument that everything a female offender does is a response to someone or something. She thus appears in these works as a reactive object, constrained by her gender, being acted on by other forces, be they abusive caretakers, assaultive men, or addictive substances (see Daly, 1992). The subsequent scenario of the woman propelled to crime because of gendered victimization leads to a similar agency-less, gendered path of criminality. It typically begins with her running from abuse or leaving school because of an unwanted pregnancy and ends with her on the street doing the only thing her gender allows (i.e., prostitution) to obtain drugs, which she uses solely to numb the pain of her past (Daly, 1992). Although later scholarly treatments accorded women a bit more

---

[1] As stated in Belknap (2007, p. 33), Lombroso and Ferrero's book, *The Female Offender,* was published in Italian in 1893 and translated into English in 1895.

19

agency with framing gender-deviant behaviors (e.g., violence, gang activity) as being a form of resistance to patriarchal and racial oppression, they still appear overly deterministic with their sole emphasis on gender (see J. Miller, 2001).

In the second characterization, women offenders are represented as "sisters in crime" or "dangerous street feminists, blazing a trail of equality through their adoption of violence and aggression" (J. Miller, 2001, p. 1). Scholars of this persuasion argue that these newly reconfigured women have appeared for a variety of social and economic reasons, from a supposed change in the meaning of *gender* on the streets and the appearance of new models in place of conventional old ones to the loss of inner city men to prison. The latter has supposedly opened up a wealth of criminal opportunities for women who, because of the former, are more than ready and willing to step up and become the 21st century's new criminal and drug entrepreneurs (see Sommers, Baskin, & Fagan, 2000).

Much of the literature that has explored female criminality continues to fall between these two poles with respect to the characterization of women and their capability for volition—or, as Lisa Maher (1997) argued, it remains informed by two distinct approaches. The first approach, by focusing solely on their gendered victimization in a patriarchal society, denies women any choice or self-determinations, and the second approach, by ignoring the effects of gender marginalization, overendows them with such agency (p. 1). Moreover, both approaches, which frame and reduce women's actions to being bound by or a product solely of their gender, "essentialize behavior rather than [providing an] understanding [of] its complexities" (J. Miller, 2001, p. 11). They deny, in other words, not only the "variations in [individual] women's experiences" (J. Miller, 2001, p. 10) but also the possibility that some degree of similarity or "shared circumstances in life" (J. Miller, 2001, p. 15) may cross gender lines and underlie the behaviors of both men and women.

In the literature review that follows, I examine the scholarship on women and crime with the preceding observations in mind. It is a focused review in which I discuss the bodies of work that were instrumental in shaping my thinking during this inquiry. In addition to the previously mentioned etiological literature, which speaks to the background causes of women's involvement in crime, I also review scholarship that is more psychological in nature and addresses deeper motivational questions about criminal behavior. My interest in doing so was to understand what crime seemed to mean to my research participants. Accordingly, I wanted to know something about "those aspects in the foreground of criminality that make its various forms sensible, even sensually compelling, ways of being" (Katz, 1988, p. 3), within the context of certain life courses. Also, to establish this context or set the stage for those who performed crime on it, I briefly discuss literature associated with urban sociology, especially that of Anderson (1990, 1999), Bourgois (2003), and Wilson (1997).

FEMINIST PATHWAYS RESEARCH

Advocates of the *pathways approach,* as used by Belknap (2007), attempt to understand and "sequence the major events in girls' and women's lives" (p. 71) that result in a trajectory to crime. Research in this tradition continues to indicate that primary among these events or forces in the women's course to criminality are childhood trauma and adult relational abuse and trauma.[2] Thus, the theoretical challenge and distinguishing theme of pathways literature is, as Daly (1992) wrote, filling the "black box" between victimization and criminalization (p. 49). As discussed earlier, the trend in the literature has been to fill this box in one of two ways: either (a) with activities that are the outcome of events beyond the woman's control, which are then cast as survival strategies or as a form of resistance to male oppression, or (b) with actions freely initiated by the woman in response to her situation or environment.

When working within the pathways tradition, the strategy used to contextualize the link between the two variables of victimization and criminalization has been characterized as "quasi-longitudinal" (Belknap,

---

[2] Estimates vary about the incidence of prior histories of physical, sexual, and emotional abuse and neglect among women offenders. However, Owen (1998) asserted that "physical and sexual abuse is a defining feature in the lives of many women in prison" and that among her sample of 300 female inmates in California "80 percent . . . indicated some type of abuse at any time in their lives" (p. 43). Moreover, 71% of her sample reported ongoing physical abuse under the age of 18, and 41% reported ongoing sexual abuse. Figures for those who experienced these traumas when 18 and older were not much better: Sixty-two percent reported ongoing physical abuse, and 40% reported ongoing sexual abuse (p. 43).

2007, p. 70); that is, unlike pure longitudinal research, in which data are collected from individuals over time, this type of inquiry accesses retrospective data from research participants at one point in time; in other words, the individual girl or woman is asked to reflect on past events that explain her current status in life. From these interviews the researcher typically constructs life histories or biographies that, to the greatest degree possible, incorporate the woman's own voice as to the meanings made of significant events and people in her life course.

Early Pathways Literature

Particularly representative of the early pathways approach is Gilfus's (1992) widely cited research, which conceptualizes women's involvement in illegal activities as beginning with survival strategies borne of interpersonal violence that become an "immersion," rather than "career" progression, into further "street work" because of "distorted notions of relational and caretaking obligations" (p. 85). Using in-depth life history interviews of 20 incarcerated women age 20 to 41, Gilfus examined the different strategies of the participants' lives, from childhood through adolescence to adulthood, to offer a distinctive framework for understanding their progression from victim, to survivor, to offender.

Victimization became linked to criminalization and the boundaries between the two blurred, Gilfus (1992) argued, as young women who were the products of families marked by "an overwhelming amount of violence" became involved in street-level illegal work "simply in order to survive" (p. 85). It was these same early experiences of violence, Gilfus said, that socialized women with "highly gender stereotyped identities centered around distorted notions of relational and caretaking obligations," which both motivated and restrained their subsequent criminal activities (p. 85).

On the basis of the dominant themes that emerged from her interviews of "violence, loss, and neglect with a strong sub-theme in which [the women] portrayed themselves as caring for and protecting other family members," Gilfus (1992) thus developed a gender-specific model of what were relational patters of entry and immersion in illegal activities (p. 85). According to this model, women who have been harmed repeatedly in relationships still

22

remain committed to seek out or maintain these connections and not only conceive of themselves in terms of relational identities but also organize and define their illegal work as part of caretaking roles and responsibilities.

For Gilfus (1992), then, what appeared to distinguish and account for the differences seen in the offending patterns of men and women was the relational character of the latter, which, although tainted by histories of violence, still seemed to determine both their moral orientation to the world and the personal choices they made. Her subjects, she concluded, seemed to have sought out and found what all women were socialized to want, relational commitments, in the only arena available to them: the world of street crime. Thus, Gilfus concluded that

> Exposure to such extreme violence may socialize women to adopt a tenacious commitment to caring for anyone who promises love, material success, and acceptance, such that it represents an extreme liability for self survival and places some women at risk for becoming offenders. While women's moral orientation to caring in the abstract may appear to be an asset, in a social context of violence and an absence of the right to protection, the ethic of care appears to constrain them from initially engaging in more violent and serious crime, yet it is also that ethic, coupled with the strength of women's commitment to relationships, which seasons the women for recruitment and entrapment in illegal street work and ultimately leads to incarceration. (pp. 86–87)

Writing several years later, Ritchie (1996) presented a similar argument about how women are "compelled to crime" through her use of the concept of "gender entrapment." She began with the observation that, among the battered women she studied on Rikers Island in New York, African American women were more likely to have had a more privileged childhood family environment of feeling loved and important than their Caucasian counterparts and nonbattered African American women. She then argued that when this heightened status becomes devalued by the racism encountered through work experiences, these women seek it instead in the goal of obtaining the perfect nuclear family. Entrapped by this goal, they continue to believe that they can "fix things" (p. 105) even after the battering starts in their relationships, and they remain "held hostage" (p. 120) until self-defense is necessary or they are driven to crime to support their children and family.

Not only did Ritchie (1996) introduce variability with respect to gender identity and situational factors that mediate the relationship between abuse and criminality, but she also cast at least some of her women in a much more active and resistant frame. They in fact did not see themselves as victims, and they had strong beliefs in their own agency or abilities to better their relationships. Furthermore, when such betterment fails, or when battering begins, they had no qualms about doing what they believed they had to do to protect themselves and their families.

Similarly, Arnold (1990) argued that it is not survival strategies that start victimized African American women on the trajectory to criminality, but rather it is their resistance to continued victimization by primary social institutions and eventual dislocation from or rejection of them. Although Arnold (1990) spoke of resistance and characterized crime as a rational choice in the context of a person's dislocation from conventional institutions, her argument became no less deterministic than that of other scholars in this genre and incorporated similar gender-specific characteristics and needs that seem to have an overriding influence on the form criminality takes and the arrangements women make when engaging in it. Thus, a young girl who is victimized by patriarchal oppression in the home, racist miseducation in the school, and marginal employment in the economic sector subsequently becomes dislocated from the legitimate world; she then begins using drugs "to dull the pain of the reality of [her life]" (p. 154), engages in crime to support her drug habit, and socializes with other addicts and deviants who provide a supportive quasi-familial relationship.

E. Miller's (1986) early qualitative study of street women in Milwaukee, Wisconsin, suggested three analytically distinct paths that lead women to involvement in "deviant street networks," by which she meant "a selection of individuals mobilized in relation to specific illicit ends" (p. 35). The path taken, she wrote, varies somewhat by racial group membership, with Caucasian women the only group that seems to follow the victimization-to-crime trajectory associated with Gilfus's (1992) research. In contrast,

E. Miller indicated that African American women are more likely to be recruited into criminality through the domestic networks unique to their communities, networks that interface with those of the street in such a way that illegality is not only a part of the individual's familial history but also normatively institutionalized within the community. E. Miller's third path, which she indicated is more common among but not limited to Hispanic women, identified addiction as the reason for women's street and hustling activities (E. Miller, 1986, pp. 108–117).

Daly (1992) also found greater variability among the 40 women she studied in New Haven, Connecticut, and she introduced several different scenarios to fill in the black box between victimization and criminality, thus allowing for individual differences in the motivation for and meaning of crime. Only one of these pathways to crime conforms to what she stated is the leading feminist perspective or "street woman scenario" represented by the works of E. Miller (1986) and Gilfus (1992). Instead, Daly (1992) identified five categories of women: (a) street women, (b) harmed-and-harming women, (c) battered women, (d) drug-connected women, and (e) "other" women. Although she noted similarities and considerable overlap between the histories and life experiences reported by women within these groups, Daly also was able to distinguish among the different categories by noting specific features common to the women in each group. Most important in effecting this grouping was the level of psychological and physical harm experienced by the women in past victimizations.

Among pathways, works that incorporate more of a macrosociological focus by stressing community-level structural arrangements and processes conducive to crime or determinative of its patterns are those by Chesney-Lind and Rodriguez (1983); Goldstein, Ouellet, and Fendrich (1992); Henriques and Manatu-Rupert (2001); Johnson, Golub, and Fagan (1995); Maeve (2001); Maher (1992); Maher and Daly (1996); Maxwell and Maxwell (2000); Owen (1998); Rosenbaum (1981); and Sterk (1999). Although most of these works also start from the early life histories of victimization so common among women offenders, they contextualize these microlevel factors within cultural, structural, or economic forces to identify and explain the different life and "career" paths women take in street crime. Accordingly, they introduce somewhat more situational variability into the picture and, on the surface at least, seem less deterministic or limiting of individual agency.

Owen (1998), for example, introduced the concepts of "spiraling marginality" (p. 61) and *la vida loca* ("the crazy life"; see chap. 1, this volume) as two distinct paths that appeared to have accelerated her research participants into a street life of crime. With these concepts, she attempted to capture the impact of lives marked by victimization and economic hardships that estrange women in socially disorganized communities from conventional choices and present an "ever narrowing funneling of options" (Owen, 1998, pp. 61–62) that includes deviant activity as a reasonable survival strategy for some and an outlet of excitement for others.

Baskin and Sommers's (1998) examination of women's careers in violent crime also is illustrative of this macrolevel approach. These authors argued that it was not some commitment to an "oppositional culture" that explained the involvement in crime of their female participants; instead, they wrote that in the distressed communities where these women lived, the guardian functions of pivotal social and economic institutions have been so undermined that the women could do little but exacerbate estrangement and isolation from prosocial activities and choices (pp. 40, 41). Gone, they said, are the extended kin networks that "once acted to stave off disaster"; gone too is the stature of "old heads," church affiliations, school programs, and meaningful job opportunities that might provide an alternative or insulation from street orientations and peers. It is this context, the authors stated, that explains why so few of the women in their study saw illegal behaviors as criminal and said instead that "it was what it was . . . no more, no less" (p. 41).

Although the influence of the themes dealing with victimization and volition are apparent across the entire body of pathways research, they are particularly evident and much more characteristic of research that has used a microlevel of analysis. This is clear in the very words these works use to describe a woman's trajectory into crime; if not "criminalized," she becomes "immersed," "compelled," or "entrapped" in criminality (Gilfus, 1992; Ritchie, 1996). It also is reflected in the language used to describe a woman as an offender; she is a "survivor" (Gilfus, 1992) or is "held hostage," (Ritchie, 1996) a woman who self-medicates to deal with the trauma of abuse or hooks up with deviant street networks in search of familial relationships she has never experienced.

It is within the community of origin, instead of in terms of family and interpersonal dynamics, that these themes are played out, with somewhat less emphasis, at the macrolevel of analysis. Although relational victimization still figures prominently in these works (e.g., Owen, 1998), the woman also appears victimized by where she lives or the marginal structural arrangements available to her in the community in which she resides. She becomes the victim of "spiraling marginality" (Owen, 1998) or "engulfed in deviant street networks." Absent other resources or skills, her agency then becomes limited by "institutionalized deviance" or the presence of "illegitimate opportunity structures" (Sommers, Baskin, & Fagan, 2000), and she is represented as descending into the abyss or in search of *la vida loca*, the only source of status and excitement available to her (Owen, 1998).

Pathways Research and the Drug Scene: Equal Opportunity or Gender Restricted?

A substantial portion of more recent pathways research has been directed toward addressing women's involvement in the underground drug economy of American cities. Although most of this literature has focused on larger structural factors and social processes in explaining women's criminality, it too has been influenced by the themes of victimization and passivity versus agency, which are reframed in terms of these more macroconsiderations to provide the backdrop for interpretation. Two clear theoretical divisions mark this literature.

The first theoretical division argues that the introduction of crack in the 1980s changed women's roles in U.S. drug markets and, in a sense, presented new and greater opportunities for illegal income generation (Baskin & Sommers, 1998; Baskin, Sommers, & Fagan, 1993; Sommers, Baskin, & Fagan, 1996). This equal-opportunity theme presented by the arrival of crack on the urban drug scene takes one of two forms.

The first form, represented by Bourgois (1989) and Bourgois and Dunlap (1993), is reminiscent of the works of Adler (1975) and Simon

(1975) and proceeds from the premise that women's emancipation in the larger society is now evident in "all aspects of inner-city street life" (Bourgois, 1989, pp. 643–645), including the structural arrangements associated with the street-level drug economy. Accordingly, the argument is made that instead of facing "exploitation in the entry-level job market," more women "are pursuing careers in the underground economy . . . [where] they seek self-definition and meaning through participation in street culture" (Bourgios & Dunlap, 1993, p. 122).

In contrast, the second form directs attention to the "macro-level changes in community and drug market environments during the 1980s and 1990s" and how these have "altered women's using and selling careers" (Sommers, Baskin, & Fagan, 2000, p. 3). Three factors are identified as having "changed the dynamics and contexts of drug use and selling for women": (a) the increased availability of inexpensive and easily used but highly addictive cocaine products as an alternative to heroin; (b) the structural shifts in the social and economic composition of inner cities, marked by the disappearance of males to imprisonment and loss of legitimate job opportunities; and (c) a market for cheap cocaine products in which demand exceeded the capacity of existing drug distribution systems (pp. 3, 5).

What at first seems to underlie both of these models is the image of a new woman, one who is unrestrained by traditional gender roles and expectations and who appears to be presented with, and rationally chooses, a viable career path in a cocaine economy no longer dominated by men. Accordingly, Sommers et al. (2000) asserted the following:

> Viewing women's involvement in drug markets in economic and career terms suggests an active role in decision-making. Earlier deterministic conceptions of women and drugs described a passive drift into the secondary roles of hustling and prostitution in a street world dominated by men. However, the accounts provided by [these] women indicate that within contemporary drug markets, women made decisions to enter based on a logical evaluation of career options. Here, the women considered both economic (wages) and non-pecuniary (status) returns from work in the secondary labor market. Furthermore, they realistically assessed their chances of obtaining economic and social support from domestic arrangements. Recognizing their con-

strained options, these women opted for illicit work which to them seemed to represent a rational choice. (p. 83)

The themes of victimization and lack of agency re-emerge, however. This is true even within the works of Bourgois and Dunlap (1993, p. 123), for instance, who argued that the breakdown of traditional patriarchal relations has taken place at a faster rate on inner city streets than in middle-class suburbs. In spite of this supposed change in urban culture, Bourgois and Dunlap simultaneously maintained that "traditional gender relations still largely govern the street's underground economy" and that "women are forced disproportionately to rely on prostitution to finance their habits" (p. 123). It is within this world of prostitution, which has been "decimated by the flood of nonprofessional, freelancing youth who are scrambling for a vial of crack," that the crack-using woman is now victimized both economically and physically, and, it is because of her addiction to crack that she now loses all agency, becoming "desperate" and "thirsty," and is derisively represented solely in terms of her drug use as a "crack whore" (p. 123).

Similar outcomes are described in the work of Sommers et al. (2000), as their rational, career-seeking new woman progresses or becomes immersed in the life and world of crack. Within this context, the drug (crack) replaces relational abuse, and the woman is now a victim of what was her previous opportunity. Because of her addiction, she is driven to "chase the pipe" and, as a result, reconfigures her social and economic life to accommodate drugs, with all friends, income, and status derived from participation in street networks that support her addiction. Moreover, she comes to see and think of herself as a victim of drugs, as a "crackhead" or "coke bitch," with "any notion of a 'calculus' [or rational decision making, gone] and 'chasing the pipe' [becoming] the one and only goal of life" and sole justification for any deviant behavior she commits (p. 85).

These same themes of victimization and lack of volition also are apparent in the opposing body of literature, which argues there has been a continuity of gender-restricted opportunities in the street-level drug economy (Goldstein et al., 1992; Inciardi, Lockwood, & Pottieger, 1999; Maher, 1997; Maher & Daly, 1996; Maher, Dunlap, Johnson, & Hamid, 1996). Maher and Daly's (1996) work is highly representative of this perspective.

In reviewing earlier literature on women in the drug economy before the advent of crack, Maher and Daly (1996) cited four elements that restricted gender equality in the roles of selling and distributing drugs: "intimate relationships with men, the availability of alternative options for income generation, restrictions on discretionary time, and institutionalized sexism in the underworld" (p. 466). Testing these factors in their ethnographic study of more than 200 women drug users conducted during 1989 through 1992 in the New York City neighborhood of Bushwick, Maher and Daly found institutionalized sexism to be the most potent explanatory variable for what they claim is continuity in the lack of opportunities for women in the drug market.

On the basis of their findings of fieldwork in Bushwick that no woman interviewed was a business owner and just one worked as a manager, Maher and Daly (1996) interpreted the relegation of female employees to the lowest levels of drug selling or as temporary workers by examining the requisite human qualities associated with the performance of pivotal roles within the drug economy. It is, they claimed, the possession of these qualities or traits, such as capacity for violence, courage, and loyalty, which are primarily gender based, that determine opportunities for income generation in the street-level drug economy and that reproduce sex segregation and institutional sexism in the underworld (Steffensmeier, 1983; Steffensmeier & Terry, 1986). Accordingly, Maher and Daly concluded, women are not thought to be as bad as men, and because men incorporate "gendered displays of violence" in their work routines, they "not only cement their solidarity as men, but also reinscribe these traits as masculine. . . . As a consequence, men are able to justify the exclusion of women from more lucrative 'men's work' in the informal economy" (p. 477).

In this literature, then, the woman becomes a victim of her gender and is unable to progress to more lucrative positions in the drug economy because she encounters "employers' perceptions of [women] as unreliable, untrustworthy, and incapable of demonstrating an effective capacity" (Maher & Daly, 1996, p. 478). The woman in these works becomes further victimized by the economic devaluation that crack has had on her main illicit activity (i.e., prostitution), and she now is a slave not to the pimp but to the pipe. Also, much more so than her male drug-using counterpart, she is represented to the world in terms that both condemn her violation of gender role expectations and chastise her lack of control and agency. She becomes, as Lisa Maher (1992) wrote, the "crack ho," "crack mom," "monster," or "antimother," who is "sexually promiscuous, selfish, and unwilling to forsake her own desires for the nurturance of others" and, as such, is "the ideal candidate for social control and punishment" (p. 136).

Contrasting interpretations are provided by research in which gender is considered in the context of its meaning to the individual person, her background, skills, and racial identity, as well as her particular social time and place. Examples include the works by Denton and O'Malley (1999), Dunlap and Johnson (1996), Maher (1996, 1997), Maher et al. (1996), Mieczkowski (1994), and Morgan and Joe (1997).

Mieczkowski (1994), for example, found different role types among women drug dealers that varied from each other in terms of their degree of independence or dependence on male partners or associates. He further found that women moved between these roles during the course of their involvement in the drug-selling subculture. Moreover, although Mieczkowski observed gender-based differences between crack dealers, specifically with respect to how women managed violence and exploitation by men in the market, he also uncovered characteristics that were uniform across the genders.

Primary among these were women's opportunistic reasons for getting involved in drug dealing or, as Mieczkowski (1994) wrote, drug dealing for these women was a mode of surviving that represented a variation on a class of hustling activities they had already pursued. Driven by choice, necessity, or a combination of both, to be independent, to make one's own way in life, led to the decision that, like many other hustles, drug dealing was simply a good way to "get over." In this regard, Mieczkowski concluded, the women reflected a choice pattern that was indistinguishable from the men in his study (p. 232).

Denton and O'Malley's (1999) findings also challenge those of other researchers who place women at a disadvantage in the drug market because of a lack of male attributes centering on violence and ruthlessness. Instead, what Denton and O'Malley found as a crucial resource for successful women drug dealers was "a variety of [relational] skills often associated with women in a disparaging fashion" (p. 528), an orientation and social skills linked to women's roles in sustaining family and kin relations on which they relied in securing core business partnerships and a style of dealing that stressed one's reputation for honesty, dependability, fairness, and trust. Although ruthlessness and violence were also within the women's "repertories of action" (p. 513), Denton and O'Malley stressed the peripheral importance of these skills as opposed to "another key resource" (p. 528): business acumen (pp. 513, 528). It is this latter gender-neutral skill that figured prominently in Morgan and Joe's (1997) study of the economic roles and drug use careers of women methamphetamine users and sellers in Hawaii and on the West Coast.

Advancing more of a cross-cultural, contextual analysis that takes into account the distribution and use patterns associated with different drugs, Morgan and Joe (1997) advocated a move away from a "traditional gender-based [examination] of women in the illicit drug economy" (p. 104). With some exceptions (i.e., Asian American women and Asian Pacific women, whose participation within the methamphetamine economy is linked to kinship and extended family networks), Morgan and Joe reported that there is a "declining significance of males for women in the illicit drug economy" and that the primary determinants for success in that sphere "were not much different from women in the legal realm" (p. 104). They stated that women in their study who achieved "long term and substantial economic success" in the drug economy were those who evinced personal discipline and were "able to maintain steady control over their [own] drug use . . . [and] tended to [have] higher education, status and greater job skills" (p. 106).

Finally, Dunlap and Johnson (1996) documented the importance of other human resources provided by family and kin networks on the development of a successful crack seller's career. Within the context of a gender, race, and class analysis, they detailed the life history of Rachel, a 20-year marijuana and crack seller, who was raised in an extended African American family in New York City's Harlem, with an ambitious, conventional grandmother as her primary caregiver and an alcoholic mother for whom she (Rachel) served as protector and nurturer. The presence and influence of the moral, social, and cultural resources provided through her upbringing were critical not only in shaping the nature of Rachel's sub-sequent involvement in crack sales but also in enabling her to develop and maintain a conventional identity while engaged in this career. She selected her customer base carefully, selling only to "normal"-looking older indi-viduals, "who held jobs . . . and cared about their appearance" (p. 185), thus bringing "to the inner city crack experience a form of controlled use" (p. 190) and order that kept law enforcement away from both her and her customers.

LOOKING BEYOND GENDER FOR CRIMINAL MOTIVATION

Gender in a patriarchal society such as that of the United States certainly matters in creating potential criminogenic conditions for women. At the same time, however, one must acknowledge that women who become the clients of the criminal justice system are the products of, or are marginal-ized by, much more than their gender. They are, in fact, the victims of multiple marginalities or " 'triple jeopardy' . . . in that their gender, race, and class have placed them at the economic periphery of society" (Owen, 1998, p. 41). Thus, I argue that these women's life courses should be exam-ined not only within the context of gender but also with a close eye toward other marginalities, which together shape their life chances as well as their thought processes and outlook on life. Although several of the pathways works I have reviewed in the preceding paragraphs consider the effects of social, structural, and economic conditions on women's progression into crime, the intersection of these conditions with gender in shaping what might be considered deviant motivational states is less evident and more the focus of the literature that follows.

By using such expressions as "thought processes," "outlook on life," and "deviant motivational states," I am suggesting a different look at women's involvement in crime through the use of a more powerful lens that enables an examination of individual-level factors and processes (McGuire, 2004, p. 30). In other words, like Katz (1988), I see the useful-ness in turning my attention to the foreground of criminality, in addition to its background of larger societal influences associated with trajectories or pathways to crime. What I seek, in other words, is the offender's perspective on the process of committing crime or an understanding of crime "through the eyes of those who commit [it]" (Wright & Decker, 1994, p. 3). What leads to the crime? What events, actions, thinking precede it? What is its motivation or meaning to the offender, and can these be discerned in the manner in which the crime is accomplished?

I should emphasize that such a focus in no ways implies the ignorance of larger social and economic considerations; instead, it directs attention to some very real consequences of these forces on the individual person, her outlook on life, her sense of and belief in the self, and the meanings she attaches to what she does or has been done to her. Like Wright and Decker (1994), I believe that an understanding of the offender's perspective is of critical importance to theory formulation, because it enables one to link factors associated with lawbreaking to crime through the perceptions and decision-making processes of offenders (p. 3). In other words, as Hans Toch (1987, as quoted in Wright & Decker, 1994) stated, "criminology can benefit by illuminating the 'black box' (offender perspectives) that intervenes between conventional independent variables (criminogenic influences) and dependent variables (antisocial behavior)" (pp. 3–4).

Several themes thought to be relevant to the individual offender's decision making, thought processes, and motivational states are suggested by pertinent literature. These are highlighted in the sections that follow. However, before I undertake that discussion it is first necessary to understand the larger social and economic world in which these themes are grounded and nurtured, or what has been called "the world of the new urban poor" (Wilson, 1997). I therefore first address a brief review of literature that describes this cultural or ecological context.

THE ECOLOGICAL CONTEXT FOR CRIMINAL MOTIVATION

In an examination of what he called the "new urban poverty," Wilson (1997) drew attention to the existence of a new ghetto environment in the United States, one in "which a substantial majority of individual adults are either unemployed or have dropped out of the labor force altogether" (p. 19). He noted at the inception of his argument that "a neighborhood in which people are poor but employed is different from a neighborhood in which people are poor but jobless. The consequences of high neighborhood joblessness are more devastating than those of high neighborhood poverty" (p. xiii).

To understand the effects of joblessness on today's ghetto residents, Wilson (1997) advocated the use of a broader vision that integrates social structural and cultural variables with social psychological factors, the last of which, he stated, have generally been ignored in previous works (p. xiv). All of these forces are examined within the context of the disappearance of work, and the resulting interpretation speaks to both the relative significance of each as well as their interactive dimensions "in determining the experiences and life chances of [today's jobless] inner city residents" (p. xiv).

For instance, when Wilson (1997) entertained the structural concept of social disorganization within the "jobless ghetto" he found a relatively high degree of social integration (i.e., local neighboring but isolation from contacts in the broader mainstream society) and low levels of social control (i.e., feelings of control over one's immediate environment; Wilson, 1997, p. 63). The result, he wrote, is a doubling of disadvantage for the children and adolescents in the area: They are at risk not just because of the lack of informal controls but also because the interactions they do have, although useful for disseminating information that is helpful for existence in the ghetto milieu, are far from effective in promoting their welfare in society at large (pp. 64–65).

Similarly, when Wilson (1997) examined ghetto-related ways or culture in areas with high rates of unemployment, he indicated that they are far more potent than in stable economically marginal areas where community members are still employed, even if at minimum wage levels, because in these areas ghetto-type behaviors are more frequently manifested and tolerated. Within this context, they are to some extent situationally adaptive, according to Wilson, and are given some measure of apparent legitimacy:

> The decision to act in ghetto-related ways, although not necessarily reflecting internalized values, can nonetheless be said to be cultural. The more often certain behavior such as the pursuit of illegal income is manifested in a community, the greater will be the readiness of

some residents of the community to find that behavior not only convenient but morally appropriate. They may endorse mainstream
norms against this behavior in the abstract but then provide compelling reasons and justifications for this behavior, given the circumstances in their community. (p. 70)

Finally, Wilson (1997) introduced a social psychological concept into
his examination of the meaning of joblessness in inner city ghettos, that
of perceived self-efficacy drawn from social cognitive theory. He used this
concept to refer "to beliefs in one's own ability to take the steps necessary
to achieve the goals required in a given situation" (p. 76), and he indicated
that the sense of inefficacy is more likely to take root and become a cultural problem of self-beliefs and collective beliefs within the jobless ghetto
because of the numbers of unemployed and the lengths of time they are
without work. More specifically, Wilson stated,

> In the more socially isolated ghetto neighborhoods, networks of kin,
> friends, and associates are more likely to include a higher proportion
> of individuals who, because of their experiences with extreme eco-
> nomic marginality, tend to doubt that they can achieve approved
> societal goals. . . . The longer the joblessness persists, the more likely
> these self doubts will take root, [making it reasonable to assume] that
> the association between joblessness and self-efficacy grows over time
> and becomes stronger the longer a neighborhood is plagued by low
> employment. (p. 76)

Anderson (1990), like Wilson (1997), directed his attention in the
classic *Streetwise: Race, Class, and Change in an Urban Community* to the
impact that social and economic disinvestment has had on life and lives
in urban ghettos. Contemporary deindustrialization or the loss of industrial and manufacturing jobs in the cities has stressed the moral fabric of
America's inner cities, Anderson (1990) claimed, and "the interpersonal
trust and moral cohesion that once prevailed [have been] undermined
[and replaced by] an atmosphere of distrust, alienation, and crime" (p. 3).

A significant casualty of these changes has been the "old heads," the
once-respected law-abiding elders of both genders; they and the stabilizing
influence of their presence on the community are no longer valued in this

context of sorely limited employment opportunities. Replacing them in what Anderson (1990) called the "cultural manifestation of persistent urban poverty" is the antithesis of the "new old head," an individual who "derides family values" and "makes ends meet . . . in the drug trade or some other area of the underground economy" (p. 3). What now directs public social relations or underlies this cultural manifestation of persistent urban poverty is, Anderson (1999) later argued, a "code of the street." By this he meant a set of informal rules "of behavior organized around a desperate search for respect" in which individuals "build or reinforce a credible reputation for vengeance [that] is highly valued for shielding the ordinary person from the interpersonal violence of the street" (p. 10).

In his ethnographic examination of the economic and social organization of street-level drug selling in two distressed New York City neighborhoods, Fagan (1994) initially presented an argument similar to Anderson's (1990, 1999), stating that the social isolation of poor communities has skewed social norms and allowed the spread of deviant norms and values within what he wrote is a closed social system (Fagan, 1994, p. 183). At the same time, however, Fagan portrayed drug selling as a primary status-generating activity in areas where traditional job networks have been disrupted and few alternative conventional models for success are available. Fagan thus contended that the sale of drugs has had an impact on the very conception of work and the social evaluation of other economic opportunities. Moreover, he claimed that the drug economy itself has been institutionalized in distressed communities, that it has given rise to "secondary economic markets that benefit many . . . residents" (1994, p. 185), from the pool of casual labor in support of drug selling to the expansion of the prostitution industry and the flow of cash into neighborhood retail networks.

Bourgois (2003) provided an alternative interpretation of the effects associated with the restructuring of the world economy on the U.S. poor. He first noted that the "economic base of the working class has been eroded . . . [and that] greater proportions of the population are being socially marginalized" (p. 319). Then, after referencing and critiquing Lewis's (1966) culture of poverty theory of "intergenerational transmission of destructive values and behaviors within families," Bourgois (2003, p. 16) used the framework of cultural production theory to analyze the inner city street culture of El Barrio. Bourgois did not use the term *Barrio* "generically to delineate a working class Latino neighborhood." Instead, he said that *El Barrio* in New York City refers "specifically to East Harlem" (p. 352).

This culture, which has been spawned "by the cultural assault that El Barrio youths . . . face when they venture out of their neighborhood" (Bourgois, 2003, p. 8), is a "complex web of beliefs, symbols, modes of interaction, values, and ideologies that have emerged in opposition to exclusion from mainstream society" (p. 8). Bourgois (2003) characterized this culture as one of opposition and resistance that, although providing its adherents an "alternative forum for [establishing] autonomous dignity," also "embroils . . . its participants in lifestyles of violence, substance abuse, and internalized rage" (pp. 8–9), ultimately resulting in their individual destruction and community ruin.

Like Anderson (1990, 1999), Bourgois (2003) contended that the law-abiding majority of El Barrio (i.e., the old heads) have been replaced as cultural icons by the communicants of this street culture and that, having lost control of public space, these "drug-free Harlemites . . . have been pushed onto the defensive" (p. 10), unable to keep the streets away from their children without moving away from the neighborhood.

Finally, Dunlap (1992) extended Bourgois's (2003) inquiry by examining the impact of drug abuse and sales on the most important institution of these communities: family life and the larger kin network, both real and fictive. Dunlap found that the stability of both to meet family members' expressive and instrumental needs has been drastically affected by the crack epidemic. Addiction has undermined the traditional vital role played by African American women in keeping families intact, and kinship support systems have been overwhelmed by the "sheer numbers of children [who] must be cared for by the more stable households" (Dunlap, 1992, p. 203). Even more troubling, Dunlap implied, is the role now played by the latter wider kinship network in transmitting these behaviors:

> It is almost impossible for children growing up in these families to define themselves except in relation to the world of drugs that surrounds them. [What once rescued them from a drug orientation, the wider kin network], now only reinforces it and helps to isolate the individual further from "mainstream" influences. (p. 204)

At the beginning of this section, I stated that several themes in the literature seem to offer potential insight for understanding the structural and normative bases for decision making, thought processes, and motivational states associated with criminality. I now briefly discuss these themes within the context of the literature in which they are suggested.

The Importance of the Street to Self-Esteem and Self-Efficacy

Every work reviewed in this section sends a powerful message about what it must be like to grow up and live in today's drug-infested, violent, and jobless inner city. Demoralizing effects are felt and seen at all levels of social life, from that of the individual, who suffers assaults to his or her self-concept or sense of worth; to the family, in which economic strains and frustrations shape interactions and socialization practices; as well as the community, which is overwhelmed by a street culture that turns civility on its head. Gone in these neighborhoods is any sense of hope, future, or even escape. Instead, what is present among today's inner city residents, as Wilson (1997) stated, are low levels of social control or feelings that one can influence his or her immediate environment. Also, because both self- and collective efficacy are not possible, a sense of inefficacy is far more likely to take root or become a part of the cultural landscape in the new jobless ghettos.

Bandura (1997) defined *self-efficacy* as "beliefs in one's capabilities to organize and execute the courses of action required to produce given attainments"; also, it is this sense of efficacy, he wrote, that is "central or pervasive" to personal agency (p. 2). Moreover, the effects on a person of having or lacking a sense of efficacy are many, according to Bandura, because an individual's "level of motivation, affective states, and actions are based more on what [he believes] than on what is objectively true" (p. 2). He thus asserted,

> Such beliefs influence the courses of action people choose to pursue, how much effort they put forth in given endeavors, how long they will persevere in the face of obstacles and failures, their resilience to adversity, whether their thought patterns are self-hindering or self-aiding, how much stress and depression they experience in coping

with taxing environmental demands, and the level of accomplishments they realize. (p. 3)

Another mindset grounded and nurtured in today's jobless ghetto also has a negative impact on the sense of efficacy; this is what Anderson (1999) called a "profound sense of alienation from mainstream society and its institutions" (p. 34). He claimed that it is this lack of trust and faith "in the police . . . and others who would champion one's personal safety" that has spawned the cultural adaptation of the "code of the street" (p. 34). Unfortunately, it is only through adherence to this oppositional street culture, or by demonstrating that one can take care of oneself, that a person achieves any sense of self-efficacy or is "accorded a certain deference and regard, which translates into a sense of physical and psychological control" (p. 34). This sense of status and control is deceptive and even contradictory, however, because, as Bourgois (2003) argued, it is by "cultural practices of [violence] that individuals shape the oppression that larger forces impose upon them" (p. 17). Such expressions of violence are nothing more, in other words, than reflections of a profound "sense of internalized worthlessness" (p. 212).

In *The Fellas: Overcoming Prison and Addiction,* Terry (2003) used the concepts of alienation, low self-efficacy, and diminished self-worth to explain why heroin addicts remain mired within the world of the street. Contextualizing these ideas within the theoretical framework of symbolic interactionism, he discussed how extensive familiarity with that world, as well as frequent stays in prison, provides an individual with a sense of comfort, self-respect, and protection from further assault on the self. Thus, he argued,

> Individually, the development of the self as "bad," which is common in but not limited to [the street environment], often occurs when people are continuously treated with contempt or rejected. In [any] case, . . . respect is lacking. Conforming to the mores of the street and presenting oneself as a regular is a means of filling that void. Regarding the meaning of this respect . . . , it is a valuable form of social capital that not only serves as a means of protection but also helps form "the core of a person's self esteem, particularly when alternative

forms of self-expression are closed or sensed to be." . . . In other words, the code allows them to develop and maintain a positive self evaluation. (p. 38)

Agnew (2006) argued similarly in his discussion of why some individuals respond to life's strains, stressors, or negative emotional states through criminal (i.e., street) mechanisms as opposed to legal or conventional coping mechanisms. In noting this, however, he made an important distinction between the states of *self-efficacy* and *criminal self-efficacy,* which factors into my later discussion of this study's findings. By *self-efficacy,* Agnew referred to a person's belief that one has the ability to cope with some stress or problem encountered in one's life through legal or approved societal means, whether those means encompass problem solving with others or distracting oneself from a sense of negativity by exercising or engaging in pleasant activities (p. 88). He noted that individuals who lack such beliefs or personal resources are "more likely to engage in criminal coping" (p. 97) when they are stressed financially, emotionally, or otherwise, especially if they have a high level of criminal self-efficacy or a view of and belief in oneself as tough, street smart, and criminally adept.

The Street and High Living

As Lisa Maher (1997) observed, "the notion of 'the street' encapsulates a complex of meanings for drug users in large urban centers and inner-city residents" (p. 53). These range from the instrumental (instructive), whereby it is thought that one must master the ways of the street to survive, to the expressive, whereby the street is seen as presenting a stage for replacing the mundane routines of daily life with the risks, excitement, and celebratory atmosphere of a block party. It is with the latter meaning in mind that I discuss the street here as a motivational force for committing crime.

In the section of his book entitled "Earning and Burning Money," Katz (1988) described how chronic offenders maintain an open-ended mindset for illicit action, that they have a "mental map of social relations in deviance connections" as well as "myriad possibilities for making connections for one form of illicit action or another" (p. 214). The lure of this type of deviance, or hustling, is rooted in its qualities of action, risk, and excitement, and underlying it is an attraction, born of the street, to fast money and fast spending. As Katz wrote, "high living is done in particular ways, with particular others, and it creates social expectations that then propel the offender back toward crime" (p. 216).

Stephens (1991), likewise recognized this mindset when discussing the "cool cat syndrome" (p. 47) of the street addict role. He described the cool cat

> as one who displays little social concern or guilt for his actions, values the outward display of material goods and other signs of success, admires an easy ability to communicate in street language, values excitement, does not believe in long-term planning, condemns snitching, and generally eschews the use of violence. (p. 47)

Wright and Decker (1994) also introduced this fast-living mentality and lifestyle as a major motivational factor among individuals who had been convicted of burglary. They argued, in fact, that for many of their research participants the impetus for break-ins was not need but the status accrued by "keeping the party going" (p. 38), which meant having, displaying, and sharing street-prized symbols of hipness, drugs, alcohol, and sexual partners (p. 42).

E. Miller (1986) and others who have researched female criminality specifically (Owen, 1998; Sharpe, 2005) also noted the importance of high living and easy money to women engaged in street hustling. For E. Miller, in fact, "hustlin' and partyin'" was the stage of the female hustler's life cycle that "seemed to make street life most attractive" (p. 139). Fast money was prized among these women, she stated, not because it was easy but because of the way it made them feel and appear to others. Although E. Miller acknowledged that part of this allure entailed a desire to feel physically attractive, "to have flashy clothes and party with well-dressed men who drove long, sleek, late-model automobiles" (p. 140), she also cited other psychological and emotional motivations for the women's expressed need for the fast money of hustling. As she stated, such money was "exciting as opposed to boring," and it afforded the women opportunities not garnered with "straight work . . . to feel a sense of mastery, independence, individual accomplishment, and immediate reward" (p. 140). Furthermore, for women reared in poverty, who always had worked dead-end, low-wage jobs, having and displaying the accoutrements of fast money and living provided a means to appear "truly glamorous" (p. 140).

On the Street, Appearance Is Everything

Within the context of areas where jobs with livable wages are nowhere to be found and social relations are dictated by the code of the street there are, as Anderson (1990, 1999) called them, "new old heads" (Anderson, 1990, p. 3). Instead of being agents of the wider society, as previous old heads had been, these new role models are actors in the underground, informal economy of drugs and other criminal enterprises. As such, they send some very different (yet powerfully visible) messages about the marks of success and how one achieves them.

Many observers have noted how brand-name material possessions, ranging from eyeglasses, sneakers, boots, and clothes, to specific types of cars, are coveted by ghetto youth for what they say about their hip image, commitment to street culture, and status within the community (Anderson, 1990, 1999; Bourgois, 2003; Irwin, 1970; Wright & Decker, 1994). Anderson (1990) explained this obsession with obtaining the "cultural apparatus" associated with the "good life" as being a message of resistance with ghetto youth "repudiating the racial caste system . . . and the work ethic as it relates to work that is thought to solidify one's place at the bottom of the stratification system" (pp. 242–243). Bourgios (2003) likewise cast the clothes attached with street identity as a "refusal to accept marginalization in the mainstream . . . world" and states that these "oppositional identities . . . are both a triumphant rejection of social marginalization and a defensive . . . denial of vulnerability" (p. 158). Similarly, Katz (1988) also viewed "street styles" and the "ways of the badass" in walking, talking, and throwing one's money around as symbolic of one's complete identification with street culture and contempt of "conventional moral appeals" (p. 89).

Stephens's (1991) cool cat image of the street addict role, with its rejection of middle-class values in favor of a hedonistic lifestyle in which "money, clothes, and cars are used for image management as much as for any intrinsic worth they may have" (p. 47) was discussed earlier. Jacobs (1999) took a similar position when he noted the absence of typical middle-class concerns among those who hustle drugs:

> On the streets, conspicuous consumption is the name of the game, fueling the competitive pursuit of "personal, nonessential" items [which] become a means to an end. Such purchases demonstrate a "cool transcendence" over the financial concerns that plagues most everyone else. Through display the wearer can proclaim himself "to be someone who has overcome—if only temporarily—the financial difficulties faced by others on the streetcorner." . . . On the streets, to go cheap on one's appearance is to discount one's reputation. (pp. 30, 31)

Acting "Street" (or at Least Crazy)

A second aspect to appearance is how one projects one's physical prowess or capabilities to handle and stand up for oneself when on the street. As stated earlier, Anderson (1999) argued that the pervasive despair of today's jobless ghettos has "spawned an oppositional culture, that of 'the street,' whose norms are often consciously opposed to those of mainstream society" (pp. 32–33). This street culture conflicts with that of the predominant decent orientation of most ghetto residents, especially with respect to its "informal rules governing interpersonal behavior," in particular, which Anderson labeled the "code of the street."

Very similar to Katz's (1988) "ways of the badass," in which symbols of toughness are prized, this code directs how one should carry and present oneself on the street and how one should respond to and interact with others if tested. At its core is the primary value sought within the street-dominated ghetto, that of respect and what it does is to proscribe behaviors that challenge one of such or, as Anderson (1999) stated, it is the code that provides a "framework for negotiating respect . . . [so one] can avoid being bothered in public" by physical danger or other actions that disgrace, disrespect, or "diss" the individual (pp. 33, 34). Just as important is the outcome of demonstrated adherence to this code of prescribed behaviors: A person who successfully uses them to take care of him- or herself is "accorded a certain deference and regard, which translates into a sense of physical and psychological control" (p. 34).

Anderson's (1999) code of proscribed behaviors is presented as a "cultural adaptation to a profound lack of faith in the police and the judicial system" (p. 34). In contrast, Bourgois's (2003) concept of the "culture of terror" has been used to describe the effects of widespread, uncontrolled violence on the social environment in Spanish Harlem, which include individual isolation and profound distrust of one's neighbors (pp. 32–37). Maher (1997) referred to this culture in her ethnographic examination of sex work on the street and reported that the women in her study used several strategies to protect themselves from it. Described as necessary survival strategies, these included the projection of a "street persona" in which one "talked bad"; "acted bad"; or, as an alternative threatening stance, "acted crazy" (p. 95).

J. Miller (2001) offered a somewhat different take on the motivation for the toughness and girl-on-girl violence she heard recalled by gang girls. She recounted how these young women referred to themselves as "one of the guys" and emphasized the "importance of being tough and physically aggressive and of not being preoccupied with feminine concerns" (p. 182). To make sense of these expressions, J. Miller used the concept of "patriarchal bargain": In a social world where women are devalued, gang girls resist their own devaluation not by challenging the premises of this treatment but by defining themselves as outside of its boundaries (p. 197).

In contrast, Messerschmidt (1997) recognized the importance of viewing gender as "a situated accomplishment in which individuals produce forms of behavior seen by others in the same immediate situation as either masculine or feminine" (p. 75). In so doing, Messerschmidt claimed that gang girls adopt an identity influenced by the street culture of which they are a part: They proclaim themselves "bad girls" and demonstrate the prized behaviors of the fast life on the street, toughness, craziness, and a deep loyalty to their gang and hood (pp. 74–77).

The Hustler Outlook

Going hand in hand with a street orientation and commitment to the high living of the street is the hustler outlook on life and the people in it. Irwin (1970) described this criminal identity, who, he said in his book *The Felon,* was "a master of a distinct form" of theft. He stated that there are two major themes to hustling and those who accomplish it: "sharpness in language and intellectual skills and . . . sharpness in appearance." The former, he stated, is behind one's "ability to dupe, to outwit through conversation," and the latter, with its emphasis on expensive clothes and cars, is crucial to the slick, smooth image or front one wishes to project (p. 12).

The hustler's worldview, Irwin (1970) wrote, is that

> the world is made of those who take and those who are taken. They did not make it this way, [it is just the way it is], so the sensible course . . . is to be one of those who takes and try to keep others from taking from you. (p. 15)

Samenow (2004) was far less kind in his descriptions of the thinking characteristic of these types of offenders, who he stated are "liars . . . behind a mask a secrecy . . . with inflated self-images" (p. 98), constantly scheming and unable to see people or property as nothing more than "opportunities for conquest" (p. 84).

In comparison, Jacobs (1999) situated hustling or "getting over" as "the conduct norm" or "one of the strongest of drug market prescriptions" today (p. 68). He claimed that it is most pronounced for "hardcore, street-level crack users—given their compulsive use and advanced stage of addiction" (p. 68). Also, instead of a form of deceit or lying that serves no purpose other than acquisition, Jacobs conceptualized getting over as a "skill and fine art," or even a sense of personal capital that earns the person "an elevated status of sorts" and, more important, a "public construction of self respect" (p. 68).

In contrast, Messerschmidt (1997, p. 42), in his analysis of the varied life history of Malcolm X—particularly during the years when he was known as "Detroit Red," a "zoot suit hipster hustler"—described hustling as a means by which a specific race and class masculine identity is constructed within a particular social context. He argued, in other words, that hustling for fast money became the means by which Malcolm X and others in his immediate race, class, and social situation accomplished gender or "did masculinity" (p. 55).

Maher (1997) built on Messerschmidt's (1997) idea of crime being a means of doing difference (i.e., demonstrating or constructing one's gender identity within particular racial and socioeconomic contexts) when she examined how gender often influences one's access to criminal and unlawful hustling activities, both of which, she stated, are identified by drug users as "street hustles" (Maher, 1997, p. 108). Maher defined *criminal hustles* as activities that are against the law, such as street crime, and she defined *unlawful hustles* as acts of income generation within the informal economic sector or work performed "under the table" (p. 109). She observed how even within the hustling world of the street, "constructions of work . . . are both raced and sexed . . . [reflecting] broader social and economic inequalities" (p. 127). Maher found, in other words, that women continued to be constrained in access to criminal and unlawful opportunity structures by attitudes and stereotypes about their gender.

But Crime Is Fun

In 1969, John Lofland wrote that it was possible "to entertain the notion that human beings are . . . capable of a positive sense of adventure, of excitement and of enchantment and that such experiences can be associated with, or even generated by, acts of deviance" (p. 104). Having said this, he added that "there may be . . . [in fact] a rather powerful demand for the pleasantly fearful among humans" (p. 104). Lofland, then, argued that it was possible to derive from deviant acts or crime a sense of *pleasant fearfulness,* by which he meant manageable excitement, challenge, fun, or adventure, in several ways. The first is when one derives a sense of winning or "getting over" someone with the commission of the deviance, that it was a game or contest of social skill at which one was successful. The second involves the adventure one feels at being daring or "making an excursion into the forbidden" (p. 107). The final quality associated with deviance that might yield pleasant fearfulness is that which results

from doing the prohibited act itself, as in the case of drugs or sexual practices (p. 109).

Katz (1988) is perhaps best known for his elaboration of these ideas
about the fun, adventure, and excitement in doing deviance in his work
Seductions of Crime, in which he advocated focusing on the foreground of
crime, not its background factors, to understand the immediate motivation
or reasons behind the activity. The challenge, Katz argued,

> is to specify the steps of the dialectic process through which a person
> empowers the world to seduce him to criminality.... We must
> explain how the individual conjures up the spirit.... [and] we must
> accept the attraction or compulsion [to crime] as authentic. (p. 7)

A significant element of that attraction, he argued, is the "sneaky thrill"
(pp. 52–73) experienced by the offender after "the scene of risk is successfully is exited," and that thrill results, according to Katz, not just from the
acquisition of "things" but with getting away with something that is
"shameful" and shame-yielding. Accordingly, he argued,

> Success brings in its wake emotions that go far beyond the joy of
> material acquisition. The "it" in "getting away with it" is not just the
> object, but something significantly shameful. Thus, the other side of
> the euphoria felt from being successful is the humiliation from being
> caught. What the sneak thieves are avoiding, or getting away with not
> being caught, is the shame they would feel if they were caught.... To
> these young thieves, being caught is an experience of degradation.
> Just as success can bring a thrill to one's entire being, so failure can
> threaten one's moral existence. (pp. 64–65)

Stephens (1991, p. 45), citing Rosenbaum (1981), described "the
attraction of the fast-moving and exciting lifestyle to neophyte heroin
users. They were frequently busier—in learning to cop, to hustle, to shoot
drugs—than they had ever been in their lives." Also, citing Hanson,
Beschner, Walters, and Bovelle (1985), Stephens described the street
addict subculture as one of "great excitement," and at times "provoca-
tive and captivating," providing several rewards (at least to new users),
including

> [the] thrill of being on the street where by pursuing heroin, they also
> chose adventure and excitement; . . . a sense of approval from their
> peers, and, if the hustling was successful, a feeling of mastery over
> particular skills; and . . . a feeling of relief, escape or empowerment
> which accompanies the effects of heroin, while simultaneously expe-
> riencing the distress and complications of heroin use. (Stephens,
> 1991, p. 45)

Sharpe (2005) likewise described the early days of the crack scene, before it turned "ugly," as being one "endless party" for her respondents (pp. 98–99). Elements of the fun, excitement, and possible status resulting from drug and other risk-taking hustles have been stressed in many other works (e.g., see Jacobs, 1999; Stephens, 1991; Wright & Decker, 1994). Whereas Agnew (2006), for example, has noted their strain-relieving properties, E. Miller (1986) emphasized their normative bases, and J. Miller (2001) discussed their role in relieving boredom.

Finally, Wright and Decker (1994, p. 160) extended Katz's (1988) line of thinking beyond amateurs or the young, novice thief and argued that even seasoned offenders, who typically "view the threat of apprehension as 'just another cost of doing business'" are not insulated "from the euphoria that follows a successful theft." Although among some offenders, the reasons for such feelings were clearly related to the "threat of being shamed" (Wright & Decker, 1994, p. 160), other offenders felt relief at avoiding a probable stiffer sentence because of their lengthy records.

Distorted Families and Their Defensive Worldview

Fleisher (1995, p. 104) moved from the street to the distorted families it produces and made a more social psychological argument about the defensive worldview that develops in children who are raised in households characterized by neglect, abuse, and addiction. He stated that this way of perceiving and interpreting one's social world is distinguished by six traits: (a) a sense of vulnerability and need to guard oneself, (b) a lack of trust in others, (c) the maintenance of social distance, (d) a reliance on violence to rebuff others, (e) an attraction to others with the same outlook, and (f) an expectation that no one cares or will provide help in times of trouble.

One can recognize this outlook on life, Fleisher (1995) argued, in the behaviors of individuals who subscribe to it. These include, he stated, an "emphasis on self-protection, suspicion, impulsiveness, insensitivity, reliance on physical force, propensity for risk-taking . . . , and a reluctance to become socially intimate" (p. 104). Fleisher then identified these traits as similar to Gottfredson and Hirschi's (1990) indicators of low self-control and, thus, an outcome of poor socialization or, as he called it, "defective enculturation" (Fleisher, 1995, p. 106).

Fleisher (1995) stated that in childhood these traits function as survival skills: "A defensive worldview enables youngsters threatened by forces outside their control to protect themselves; they withdraw, become aggressive, act moment to moment, and distrust adults (potential abusers)" (p. 105). As the children age, however, and enter the larger social world of schools and jobs, these behaviors become maladaptive and isolate them from potential positive, counteractive interactions with teachers and peers who cannot cope with the demonstration of such behaviors. Also, as adolescents, once they start to get labeled as delinquent and removed to detention facilities, their opportunities for normal interactions and experiences become further truncated and their social maturation is "retarded," leaving them in a "prolonged state of adolescent dependency" (p. 105).

Accompanied by a set of "sociocultural and sociolinguistic grammars . . . outside its carrier's awareness," this defensive worldview places individuals at a disadvantage in interpreting social situations, and as a result they are unaware of miscues as they "say the wrong things and behave badly." Moreover, Fleisher stated, this defensive worldview passes "from adults to children within generations of family culture in the process of enculturation: [Defensive] parents who perceive rejection by their children will automatically react with hostility, often leading to rage and violent behavior when they beat their children" (Fleisher, 1995, p. 106).

The distorted family relationships responsible for the worldview Fleisher (1995) described can be contextualized easily within what Agnew (2006, pp. 51–70) identified as those strains most likely to result in coping strategies that involve criminal activity because they are high in magnitude, seen as unjust, associated with low social control, and create some pressure or incentive for criminal coping. Agnew stated that the relationship between parental rejection, neglect, and abuse and children's delinquency and criminality is well established in the literature and seems to operate through the strong negative affective states it engenders in children as well as the loosening of any moral and social constraints against deviance. Moreover, when treated brutally and unjustly by caregivers, the children not only lose their attachment to these parental and other conventional figures but also suffer the loss of concern for others in general, and the belief that deviance and or "getting up" on others seems to become justified.

The Street as a Stage for Expressing Shame, Anger, Guilt, and Other Traumas of Life

For a number of the women I interviewed, the street and what they did on it appeared to have deep psychological meaning. In many ways, in fact, it seemed to offer them a stage on which they could express and, at times, exorcise the demons associated with their pasts of neglect and abuse. This characterization certainly did not apply to all of the women. Instead, it was primarily associated with those who had been profoundly harmed, psychologically or emotionally, in highly dysfunctional and usually combative families and those who had preexisting conditions that impaired their abilities to accommodate such stressful households.

Indeed, the intense effects of personal trauma were expressed throughout my interviews of the women who are the focus of this book. Among those who had been abandoned or neglected by mothers, for instance, there was often a great deal of emptiness expressed, accompanied by feelings of alienation (Meares, 2000, p. 56). In fact, one woman, Judy,[3] who had been rejected and made to feel unwanted by both parents, directly referred to her emptiness as the "many voids" in her life. It was these voids, she said, that she was trying to fill with her activities on the street.

Meares (2000) wrote that this emptiness is often pervasive and can be of "painful intensity" (p. 56). Moreover, because it undermines one's "sense of well-being, which is part of the 'warmth and intimacy' of [the] self, . . . it is replaced by a negative affect, . . . [which] results in a negative

---

[3] All names of the women in this study are fictitious pseudonyms.

personal evaluation" (p. 57). This evaluation might generate shame, alienation, or anger, depending on its intensity or level (Forgas & Williams, 2002; Meares, 2000; Thomas, 1993).

It should be clear how the expression of these feelings could result in behaviors that bring one trouble with the law, either by acting out in response to the feelings or by "acting in," with substance abuse, for example, to nullify their effects (Seabrook, 1993). It also has been argued (see Meares, 2000) that the preventative measures one takes to avoid these feelings in the first place—or, more specifically, to fill the emptiness that yields them—are potentially criminogenic. Thus, Meares (2000) stated that a person who has been overwhelmed by trauma and lives in a constant state of fear, even if at the unconscious level, often becomes desperate to fill the voids within the self by engaging in "stimulus seeking behaviours such as reckless sexuality, substance abuse gambling, even theft" (p. 56).

Although it also is necessary to acknowledge the role of modeling and social learning in shaping an individual's coping skills (Bandura, 1986, 1997), as well as larger structural forces, one cannot deny that for some of the women I discuss in this book upbringings of extreme emotional, physical, and sexual victimization had lasting psychic damage. Also, as readers will learn, the more these women publicly evinced behaviors associated with this damage, and were apprehended for doing so, the more they came to believe that they were nothing more than damaged themselves (Goffman, 1963; Howard & Hollander, 1997).

CONCLUDING REMARKS

The bodies of literature I have discussed in this chapter, which range from sociological and social psychological to the psychological, directed my inquiry and the interpretations I made of my findings. At the same time, however, there were several understandings and themes inherent to this scholarship that I questioned and empirically challenged with my research. I detail these thoughts in the next chapter within the context of a discussion about the basic parameters of the study I undertook.

3

The Rochester Study:
A Quasi-Ethnography of
Women Street Hustlers

Lisa Maher (1997), in her critique of early feminist research, described how the typical woman offender is portrayed:

> [She is a] passive [victim] of oppressive social structures, relations and substances, or some combination thereof. . . . Constituted by and through [her] status as victim, . . . devoid of choice, responsibility, or accountability; [a fragment] of social debris floundering in a theoretical tide of victimage. (p. 1)

Similarly, Daly (1992) discussed how in this literature the "concept of blurred boundaries" or the "seamless web of victimization to criminalization" produces "accounts which focus on victimization and leave little agency, responsibility, or meaning to women's law-breaking" (p. 48). Although later researchers certainly attempted to redress this deterministic portrayal, they likewise proceeded in the context of a gender-based framework, with assumptions about women's complete emancipation from gender restraints made because of the mistaken observation that any activity is the same thing as liberation (Maher, 1997).

The picture I developed of the women in this study was far more complex than that suggested by much of prior research. In fact, there was more than one picture generated by these women. Although some indeed appeared to be true victims—or, as Maher wrote, were constituted solely through their "victimage," with every bad thing they had ever done justified as a way to hurt someone from their pasts—there were far more who seemed to have very different motivations for the crimes they had committed. There were, for instance, women who described their daily forays into hustling as providing them with a sense of adventure or a chance to feel normal. There also were women who spoke of their current and future criminal activities as if they were part of some master business plan, with a keen sense of their potential rewards and losses over time. Finally, there were women who said the only thing they knew was hustling and that they were the best there ever was at it. Although I interpreted some of what I heard as clearly related to the gender-based experiences of the women, I also understood other remarks and observations to be genderless or common as well to the men who shared the distressed neighborhoods of origin with these women. As I considered my findings, it thus became necessary to contextualize gender in terms of its social, economic, and physical place, including these women's neighborhoods and other neighborhoods, or with race, ethnicity, and class very much in mind.

In this chapter, I provide a brief discussion of the basic contours of my research. I answer the simplest questions about the inquiry, including why I decided to pursue this research, whom I selected to participate in it, what I hoped to learn, and how I designed the research. A more complete consideration of each of these areas is presented in subsequent chapters. I also introduce in this chapter three concepts that direct the tone and content of future discussions in the book: (a) hustling trajectory, (b) hustling worldview, and (c) hustling lifestyle.

THE WHY, OR WHAT WE DON'T KNOW

I undertook this research to address what I saw as limitations in our knowledge about chronic, low-level women street hustlers. In fact, just by referring to them, the subjects of this work, as *hustlers* I am attempting to reorient the reader to both the versatility of their criminal activity and the outlook on life that seems to mark their thinking. As I discussed in chapter 2 of this volume, these qualities that shape the women's street existence are relatively muted in much of the research. I thus wanted to get beyond the stereotypes and come to understand these women as individuals who found something in their hustling street existence that had been lacking or made possible by their previous lives.

I also sought to get as close to the women's crimes as possible and to see them, if you will, through their eyes and with their meanings. Such a consideration of the offender's perspective on committing crime is relatively lacking in criminology, with some in the field going so far as to argue that theorists "are 'wasting their time' if they do not consider the mental states of criminals as they contemplate the commission of offenses" (Wright & Decker, 1994, p. 4). This lack of attention to the offender's subjective experience of crime (i.e., how decisions are made to commit an offense and what committing crime actually feels like and means to the offender) is particularly troublesome given that it usually underlies and shapes our penological practices in dealing with them.

My intent, then, was to learn about the women's mental states and thought processes or how they conceptualized of and felt about hustling before, during, and after they did it. What I wanted to know, in other words, was what crime meant to them or how they situated it in their thinking about the world, themselves, and others. Understanding this subjective reality of crime is what Lofland (1969) advised: "Deviant acts, as other acts, are connected to matters of self-esteem, threat, and adventure; to conventional patterns of social organization and participation; to mundane hardware and places; and to conventional topics of morality" (p. 116).

At the same time, however, I considered it critical to conduct this type of inquiry with the temporal dimension very much in mind. It is this perspective or sensitivity to time, I believe, that is lacking in much of the literature and that results in our many assumptions about women's involvement in crime being solely drug related and motivated. In fact, I will show that although many of the women in this study had indeed become drug addled and now were boosting (i.e., theft or shoplifting with the intent to sell; see chap. 1), engaging in prostitution, or selling drugs to maintain their addictions, they were not always like this; most of the women, in fact, had been criminally active long before they were addicted. My task, then, as I saw it, was to take these women back to their initial criminal activities and to have them speak about who they were and what they were thinking or hoping to accomplish with crime at that time.

Many questions directed my inquiry. Were these women's offenses need based, and did they have to neutralize any moral proscriptions before they drifted into crime (Matza, 1969; Terry, 2003)? In contrast, were these crimes exciting and something they enjoyed doing, a part of their lifestyle, if you will, that required no moral rationalization (Katz, 1988; Wright & Decker, 1994)? Was "acting bad" and being a "gangsta bitch" a persona required for self-protection on the street (J. Miller, 2001), or maybe even an oppositional stance to their "class and race powerlessness" (Messerschmidt, 1997, p. 70)? Finally, were these women operating with a far less flattering mindset borne of an abusive upbringing whereby they took advantage of whatever opportunity that came their way, leading meaningless lives in which crimes were nothing more than "mundane rituals" (Fleisher, 1995, p. 7)?

Just as important in directing this inquiry, and especially its potential for intervention strategies, was my interest in learning how these women interpreted their past and present worlds as well as their subjective realities of themselves, because, as recent desistance literature clearly demonstrates, offenders "need to make sense of their lives, if [they are] to successfully maintain . . . abstinence from crime" (Maruna, 2001, p. 7). Maruna explained,

> To desist from crime, ex-offenders need to develop a coherent, prosocial identity for themselves. As such, they need to account for and understand their criminal pasts (why they did what they did), and they also need to understand why they are now "not like that anymore." Ex-offenders need a coherent and credible self-story to explain (to themselves and others) how their checkered pasts could have led to their new, reformed identities. . . . The construction and reconstruction of this narrative, integrating one's perceived past, present, and anticipated future, is itself the process of identity development in adulthood. Individuals who are unable to construct this sort of consistent narrative out of their lives may suffer, depression, anxiety, . . . [and rarely make good]. (p. 7)

Terry (2003), a member of what Irwin (as cited in Terry, 2003) called "an important new community of 'ex-convict' criminologists," made similar observations, bolstered by the added credibility of having been there and done that himself (Terry, 2003, p. viii). Terry stated that turning one's life around requires a person "to undergo the difficult task of learning to see [oneself] differently" (p. 8), which among his sample of heroin addicts meant combating the negative self-concept all shared as stigmatized addicts. Terry then identified "the situations, turning points, and significant others that helped alter the meanings of things in [the lives of his sample] and the actions [they took] as a result of these changed meanings" (p. 8). It is interesting, and relevant to this study, that in his inquiry he also paired addiction with prisonization, noting the deleterious effects of the latter in reinforcing one's status as a passive, dependant, "social cripple" (p. 5).

Although I cannot say for certain, it is probably safe to assume that most of the women in this study were not at the point of reconstructing their identities to facilitate desistance from crime. However, I thought that by learning the contours of their present and past identities, and what they express about their fears, dreams, weaknesses, and strengths, I might gain an understanding of possible paths to lives free from crime. I do not believe such optimism is unfounded.

Nearly all of the women in this study had left the street at some point in their lives, hoping to reclaim children lost to the system and families who had long since given up on their daughters. Nearly all had spent time in transitional settings, halfway houses typically named after former residents who were now success stories. Finally, nearly all had also been in and out of drug treatment more often than they had been in jail, which they now said was their preferred setting for getting straight (at least for awhile). Although some of the reasons for their "failures," especially those related to securing support, housing, and employment, are well documented, others, more deeply rooted in their senses of self and feelings of competency, are not. I hope that this research will provide some insight into these unknowns.

THE WHO, OR IF NOT ON THE STREET, SHE'S IN THE JAIL

As stated earlier, the women who were the subject of this inquiry spend good portions of their lives alternating time between repeated jail stays and the street. They have been called various names in the literature, all of which attempt to capture and communicate either the route of entry by the individual into criminality—what her main activity or role in the illegal street economy is assumed to be—or society's impression, typically expressed as condemnation, of the life she is living.

As I mentioned in chapter 1 of this volume, Eleanor Miller (1986) first named these offenders "street women." Later, she and Romenesko (Romenesko & Miller, 1989) coined the more neutral expression "female street hustler," to capture the diversity and array of work in which these women engage, outside of prostitution, to survive. Daly (1992) returned to the street woman categorization but also introduced motivational elements in her criminal types of harmed-and-harming, battered, and drug-connected women. Then, in looking specifically at crack-involved women, there were Sterk's (1999) queens of the scene, hustlers, hookers, and older struggling rookies, along with Goldstein, Ouellet, and Fendrich's (1992) "skeezers." More recently, and highly reminiscent of Irwin's (1975) "rabble" and Goldfarb's (1975) "ghetto" dwellers, is Parenti's (1999) gender-neutral designation "social junk" for all street-level offenders.

As I also stated in chapter 1, to locate women for this study I went to the institution so connected with (and, in fact, reflective of) the street where they existed: a jail. The women I found there reminded me in very many ways of those written about by Elliot Liebow (1993) in *Tell Them Who I Am: The Lives of Homeless Women*, which is, I suppose, not all that surprising, given that most had been homeless in the past or were so just before their most recent incarceration. Their days and nights were structured for them, like those in a homeless shelter: They rose in the morning when "called out" for breakfast, and they retired each evening with "lights out." They spent most of their time rather bored, waiting for the next meal, card game, or cleanup, and the topics of their conversations were similar: lost property and possessions from one's past, family problems, children, religion, and acquaintances in common from the street.

I also share with Liebow (1993) some similar reactions to the individuals I met. Although at first they seemed "to be a fairly homogeneous group" (p. 16)—obviously poor women who looked worn and washed out in their unflattering green uniforms—on closer inspection they were in fact quite different from each other. Some appeared better situated than others, with friends or family members providing funds for personal items and food; others seemed very comfortable in jail, sitting at the same table with the same women doing the same things each day; still others seemed to be like ghosts, never coming out of their cubicles unless necessary or called, constantly reading with their backs to the common area. Finally, like Liebow, I enjoyed their company and was struck, from the very beginning of this study, by their quick wit and self-deprecating humor. Moreover, each day I wondered whether I would be capable of their incredible resilience and the creativity that allowed them to make do with jail provisions.

As I reflect back, it seems that my purpose in this study also was similar to Liebow's (1993), and that was to get to know these women in more than the one-dimensional or empirical terms and commonly held assumptions typically used to describe them. I had one more thing in common with Liebow: my interest in ascertaining how these women, who functioned and existed at the margins of society, "remained human in the face of inhuman conditions" (p. 1). With my background in "the system," I certainly knew that I could describe them in terms of the many demographic and health variables that have been collected more for the benefit of researchers than for theirs. What I did not know, however, and what the literature could not tell me, was how these women perceived themselves; how they constructed their pasts to explain their presents; how they did what they did criminally; and how and what they did each day criminally, and otherwise, to survive.

THE WHAT, OR FILLING IN THE BLANKS

With this research, I sought to present and interpret within existing scholarship the life course of the chronic, low-level woman offender to answer, in a longitudinal fashion, the most basic questions of who, what, where, when, how, and why. I began by situating the women within their families and communities of origin to explore and contextualize what they recounted as the most significant people, events, experiences, and relationships that underlay their movement into criminality.

I then examined the contours of that activity—its frequency, duration, development, specialization or diversity, and productivity—within the subsequent life experiences of the women (e.g., see Danner, Blount, Silverman, & Vega, 1995; DeLisi, 2002; Maruna, 2001; Piquero, 2000; Piquero & Chung, 2001). In a sense, I charted who these women were and became as offenders, and I attempted to explain the variations in careers found among them, with reference to both their personal beginnings and the community's larger criminal world of which they were a part. Finally, at the most basic, but relatively unexamined level, I explored the various interpersonal and structural resources and arrangements, both legal and illegal, that they used to survive and what that survival actually looked like and entailed. I also examined the effects, both positive and negative, of frequent jail stays on the women's lives and typically marginal existence.

A simpler way to conceptualize my research interests is to say that I sought to develop an understanding of these street hustlers in three different statuses: (a) as women (or, more specifically, as individuals whose backgrounds were examined to develop insight into their subsequent criminal involvement), (b) as offenders, and (c) as survivors. The context for this inquiry or what constituted the setting for examining their behaviors or roles in these statuses was the urban street environment.

The women who participated in this study were selected for inclusion because they had committed their offenses in this environment or were in fact urban street criminals. Most began life as inner city residents, and the small number who had not were now such because of their extensive criminal involvements. These women were low-level property, public order, and drug offenders who made their livings or generated income by both criminal activities on the street and, in many cases, somewhat unconventional but not illicit exchanges in the informal economic sector of that same environment.

The street and this neighborhood-level informal economic sector provided the context for my inquiry and very much shaped the interpretations made of the data, because in reality both were the backdrop or stage on which the women had been raised, lived, and now survived. I approached this milieu of the street, in other words, very much like Connell (1987), who characterized it not as "something we walk and drive along, or that chickens cross" but as an "institution . . . , with particular social relations" (p. 132). On one level, Connell pictures this institution as "a zone of occupation by men . . . with the same structures of gender as the family and state," where "daring, talk . . . , drugs, and sexism provide entertainment in a bleak environment" (p. 133). He also calls this environment of the street a "battleground" that serves as a scene of intimidation for women.

At the same time, however, Connell (1987) recognized the street's character as an "experimental theater" more loosely structured than other social institutions, giving "room not only to diversity, but also to quick turnover of styles" (p. 134). In fact, it could be said, at the risk of romanticizing, that when speaking of "the street" among urban residents the analogue of a mythical kingdom of Camelot proportions almost comes to mind. Although it seems to convey a lifestyle of risk, excitement, good times, and partying (Maher, Dunlap, & Johnson, 2006, p. 24), the street and its lure, like Camelot, also have an ephemeral quality and a downside from which one cannot escape. The further one goes into its lifestyle of fast money, drugs, and other hustles, the more one loses, and the less likely it is that one ever will be able to leave its hold.

Criminal activities are, of course, included within these other hustles of the street, but so too are the unconventional yet not-illicit exchanges of the informal economic sector so characteristic of impoverished urban neighborhoods and communities. As observed by others (Maher, 1997; Maher et al., 2006), low-income U.S. city neighborhoods have a long history of reliance on an informal sector of trading and exchange systems to provide goods, jobs, and services to meet the survival needs of the poor. These activities not only provide an alternative route of survival for individuals denied access to more conventional means in the formal economy but also "serve as a kind of glue which gives both form and stability to social life" (Maher et al., 2006, p. 17).

All three of the broad research interests that underlay this inquiry were contextualized in terms of these understandings of the street and its informal economic activities, both legal and illegal. Thus, in addressing the first research interest, emphasis was placed on ascertaining, through the women's reflections and perceptions, what they identified as the significant people and events that had led to and shaped their lives on the street. Personal, social, and economic information about the women's current lives, before their most recent incarceration, also was obtained, with the intent of assessing the influence of differing paths to the street on the marginal lives now experienced by these individuals.

The second research interest focused on the behavior and life course of the women as offenders. The women were first asked to list and describe the illicit activities in which they had engaged since their first arrest as an adult. They also were questioned about the reasons for offenses and any movement among different crimes, as well as any reported adherence to a particular criminal lifestyle. Once again, the street and its informal economy underlay this research interest, because the offenses in which these women engaged, primarily boosting and other property crimes, prostitution, or drug sales and possession, took place within these venues. It was thought, in other words, that their successes and failures at criminality, as well as their safety and security while so involved, might very much be influenced by the resourcefulness they had acquired to function effectively on the street; their relationships with others in that environment, from the police to their customers; and possibly shared understandings or normative expectations within the community they worked, inclusive not just of geographical boundaries but also of people and the interactions, both expressive and instrumental, between them.

As I discussed earlier, much of the literature on women's involvement in crime leaves little room for agency on the part of the offender, and in fact women often appear to have been propelled into crime by one of three things: (a) relational abuse, (b) love for a man, or (c) addiction. This deficit-based, spiraling model into the criminal abyss not only negates choice, rationality, and alternative motivations from the equation but also proceeds from a simple and arguable assumption about the relationship between drugs and criminal involvement among women, that is, that the former always precedes the latter. Moreover, it seems to obviate the possibility of change in illicit activities, because those illicit activities are assumed to be solely drug driven or a function of addiction and therefore beyond the influence of other possible personal or situational factors.

The research I present in this book challenges these themes in the literature. To begin, the existence or lack of agency was considered to be an empirical question and not assumed as being present or absent. Likewise,

I wanted to open up the discussion of causes and entertain what the women themselves had to say about their lives and behavior. In other words, I was interested in seeing through their eyes to reach an understanding of why they did what they did. Furthermore, I wanted to hear what they had to say about the drugs–crime nexus, knowing that the women were well schooled in the belief structures and language of drug treatment[1] and that their observations would be grounded in multiple sessions of self- and group reflections.

Finally, I wanted to get closer to their criminal enterprises than an etiological examination would allow. I was, as I said earlier, interested in their subjective realities of doing crime. Were there seductive elements in a situation that lured these women into crime, as Jack Katz (1988) argued? Or were they rational decision makers capable of choice? Did they identify conditions that were both necessary and sufficient for them to commit an offense? Finally, did their behavior in committing crime say anything about their underlying motivations?

My final research interest was to understand how these women survived lives marked by economic and social marginality, criminality, and the frequent interruption of jail. Such deficits are of course all too evident and certainly acknowledged to be overriding characteristics of their lives. What are not apparent and known, however, are the possible skills, means, relationships, and resources these individuals have, develop, and use to survive life on the street and in the border of that world, the jail. In other words, what I sought from the women was an understanding of these two worlds or, more specifically, their perceptions and reflections of what was available and necessary to live somewhat successfully in each. On the first level, I was interested in the ecological basis of the women's survival, both on the street and in the jail. I was curious about the people, places, and things available in these two communities that facilitated survival for the individual. Also, at the second, more personal level, I sought to assess the individual qualities and resources necessary to make this successful outcome a reality.

---

[1] Nearly every woman in this study had multiple involvements in drug court, Narcotics Anonymous, or Alcoholic Anonymous, or some form of an in- or outpatient substance abuse treatment program.

THE HOW, OR USING QUASI-ETHNOGRAPHY IN RESEARCH

This qualitative study of 60 women street hustlers is best conceptualized as quasi-ethnography (see Owen, 1998, pp. 20–22). As such, it was both similar to and different from the true or pure ethnographic approach. Paramount among its similarities was the level of understanding I sought. Owen described this as becoming privy to "domains of understanding" between persons who share some social space so as to yield a "cultural description reporting how people describe and structure their world" (Owen, 1998, p. 20). More specifically, she noted how the depth and type of information sought by ethnography has much in common with anthropology in that it uses thick (i.e., multilayered and faceted) descriptions, provided by respondents themselves, that detail the "context and meaning of events and scenes that are relevant to those involved with them" (Owen, 1998, p. 21).

Also similar to true ethnography was the method I used to collect my data, which consisted of in-depth interviews and detailed observations, as well as the analysis I made of resulting data (Owen, 1998, p. 21). The latter, like most qualitative methods, was very much influenced by symbolic interactionism and involved describing the beliefs, institutional arrangements, and normative practices of the research participants using their own voices or in terms of their specific meanings and interpretations, or, as Owen (1998), citing both Emerson (1983) and Matza (1969), observed,

> Beyond observation, ethnography involves developing an appreciation for the distinctive concerns, forms of life, and ways of behaving found in particular social worlds. . . . "[It] compels the worker to comprehend and to illuminate the subject's view and to interpret the world as it appears to him." (p. 21)

In addition to understanding how the research participants viewed their social worlds, I was even more interested in how they saw themselves, over time, and the effects these images had on their subsequent behavior (Terry, 2003, p. 11). As I said earlier, I was guided here by the basic premises of symbolic interactionism, which conceptualizes the self "as an object, like all other things . . . [that] evolves [over life in response to] new circumstances, situations, and associations with others" (Terry, 2003, p. 12).

The elements of my research that distinguished it from true ethnography are probably already apparent to readers. There are several. First, by electing to conduct this inquiry in a jail, I certainly was physically removed from that which I wanted to study: the women's social world. Thus, my ability to become fully immersed in that world (Owen, 1998, p. 21), and to "convey an inside or interior view of the phenomenon" (Matza, 1969, p. 26) in which I was interested, was somewhat hampered. Not only was my ability for close, naturalist observations limited (Matza, 1969), but also I was clearly identified as an outsider to the women in their present environment. I was "that woman writing the book" who came to the jail every day at the same time and left at shift change, when the women, like children, were restricted to their bunks as if it were naptime.

Having said this, I also must admit that, like many of the research participants, I was very comfortable in a jail setting. This comfort was borne not of time spent incarcerated but of a familiarity derived from my professional activities. I also was very relaxed around the population housed in the particular jail that served as my research site, having been raised in an inner city neighborhood of Rochester, New York, and having attended the same schools that they had at times frequented. I knew these women's streets and neighborhoods, at least from the vantage point of a resident, and in some cases we shared mutual acquaintances. I also knew a number of the women themselves from previous research conducted in this jail. It was for these reasons, as well as the unencumbered access I had to the facility, that I conducted this study where I did. For additional information and clarification of issues related to my method, readers may contact me directly at St. John Fisher College in Rochester, New York.

THE OUTCOMES: HUSTLING TRAJECTORIES, OUTLOOKS, AND LIFESTYLES

Mark Fleisher (1995) described his work on men street hustlers, the counterpart to the women who are the focus of this study, as an "emic ethnography" (p. 8). He defined this as an approach that yields understanding on several levels, beginning with the "culture or language [of a group] as an ordered whole [and progressing to] the individual actors in such a life-drama—their

attitudes, motives, interests, responses, conflicts, and personality development" (p. 8). My inquiry proceeded in a similar fashion and, in so doing,
conceptualized the women's involvement in street hustling in terms of three
phenomena directly related to my research interests: their trajectories or
pathways to the street, the outlooks they seemed to share while there, and the
lifestyle that marked their hustling existence.

I began with the life stories told by 60 women. With these stories, the
women shared with me the people, places, and things they considered significant in their life course to the street. Although at first the stories sounded
incredibly alike, with uniform recollections of poverty, abuse, and loss, after
closer scrutiny they later were conceptualized as comprising six distinct trajectories or groups (discussed in more detail later in this volume) into their
current hustling lifestyles: (a) an All in the Family group, (b) a Partiers
by Trade group, (c) a Show Me the Money group, (d) a Challenged group,
(e) a Just Another Addiction group, and (e) a Lives of Loss and Trauma
group. These trajectories were distinguished not only in terms of social
structures and processes implicated in the women's progression to crime
but also by the subjective realities of their lives or how the women seemed
to interpret their actions and motivations for doing what they did. Their
choice of words, and the sentiments they expressed when saying them, also
were a key to my analysis.

For some of the women, crime was clearly an adventure and considered fun. In fact, instead of being pushed to the street and propelled into
crime, an imagery so dominant in the literature, these women seemed
lured to the street lifestyle by the promises of fast living, easy money, and
never-ending partying that it offered. In contrast were those women who
seemed to be looking for a sense of self-esteem and control over their lives,
feelings they had never experienced—that they were, indeed, good at
something, even if it was scoring drugs and hustling just to survive. Then
there were the women who seemed like orphans looking for the ideal family, which they had sorely lacked, with whom they did everything, from
their drugs to their crimes.

I then focused on contextualizing the women's hustling outlook on
life, which was something almost all of them shared. The interpersonal
dynamics of upbringings marred by abuse certainly had much to do with

implanting the hallmarks of this perspective in their thinking. Indeed, it was very understandable why so many of these victimized women trusted no one and felt that they had to outwit others and grab what they could when the opportunity presented itself. At the same time, however, there seemed to be other, larger structural influences at work in their thinking, influences rooted in an environment mired in cultural, institutional, and economic distress.

Indeed, for most of the women it is safe to say that the conventional institutions of their early lives had been ineffective not only in socializing them but also in providing examples and incentives for pursuing a conventional lifestyle. Their families, for instance, often served to model the hustling outlook through both illegal activities and other income-generating strategies associated with the informal economic structure of the ghetto. For example, these women who now hosted house or crack parties, charging entrance fees and fees for services, had also, as children, helped mothers and grandmothers with their cocaine or basement card parties, where money was made easily and fast.

Their schools, likewise, had failed the women. For some, it was because of the lack of resources and skills in dealing with children who acted out or presented special needs. For more, it was because of the boredom and irrelevance of standard, middle-class curricula preparing them for lives that were unavailable—and, for some, unvalued—in the ghetto. When they left school, usually without graduating, their employment choices were sorely limited and lacking, especially in providing the lifestyle seen on TV that was mimicked with much flash and flair by successful drug dealers in their surroundings. Finally, there were the mistrust and alienation these women clearly felt toward the police. Borne of personal or familial experiences, they believed the police were to be avoided and that in times of trouble it was they who had to act "street"—tough or crazy—to survive.

I approached our discussions of the women's hustling lifestyle in like manner. I began with the bigger picture, interested in the ecology of it—the people, places, and things—that figured in their day-to-day lives or how they fit in their street worlds. Fleisher (1995) referred to this "collective knowledge of the street, its content, structure, and meaning" as street culture: "a logical, coherent system of adaptational rules that meet the conditions and perils of the street life and is strongly influenced by how street criminals perceive and interpret the social world surrounding them" (p. 8).

As I show in this book, there was, in fact, a certain order to the disorder of these women's street lives, with specific institutions providing for their marginal existence, norms influencing their daily activities, and beliefs shaping what can only be called an opportunistic outlook on life. There were, for instance, places they depended on early in the day for their personal needs such as a single slice of pizza or a few "loosies" (i.e., cigarettes sold individually). There also were places, or wherever people congregated, as I was told, where they could get cash for the food allowance on benefit cards or unload quickly whatever they had stolen.

There were other locations they avoided, not just because of a possible police presence but also for the threats to safety they presented. These concerns about safety also factored into the many norms associated with their specific hustling, drug use, and survival activities. Finally, there were the people in their lives, with many of whom they now sat in jail. Both they and the jail itself served certain purposes for the women, some of which were related to staying alive and others nothing more than a continuation of their present hustling lifestyle. As readers will learn, although for these individuals jail was a critical institution in providing care—or, as most said, "a place to rest"—it and its occupants often did nothing more than foster their maintenance in a street or rabble existence (Irwin, 1975).

CONCLUDING REMARKS

In this chapter, I have explained the basic contours of my research using a simple "why, who, what, and how" format. I also highlighted the understandings I sought from the inquiry, as well as those I thought I might challenge. Finally, I introduced research outcomes that parallel my interests. In the following chapters, I take a much closer, more detailed look at the "how" of my inquiry or the qualitative design I selected to obtain and analyze my data. As readers will see, the life history method I used to achieve the deep understanding characteristic of ethnographic research is rooted in both past and current sociological scholarship. Moreover, one finds its application in the earliest of American criminological research or, more specifically, the Chicago School of Sociology as well as recent feminist methods (Reinharz, 1992) and those associated with developmental criminology (Sampson & Laub, 1993). Even more promising is its use in the form of self-narratives in desistance literature (e.g., see Maruna, 2001; Terry, 2003), versions of which I introduce in subsequent chapters.

4

Designing the Research and Analyzing the Data

In the summer and fall of 2005, I became a daily visitor to the Monroe County Correctional Facility (MCF), a direct-supervision[1] local penitentiary located in a suburb of Rochester, New York. Housing inmates sentenced to 1 year and under only,[2] this facility, built in 1990, lies on a stretch of heavily traveled commercial highway and is bordered by the county medical examiner's office on one end and a community college on another. There is no fence around the jail and, unlike the county's maximum security detention facilities in downtown Rochester, it is classified as a medium security institution. Looking more like a school than a penitentiary, on both the outside and the inside, the facility consists of six large dormitory-like housing areas where inmates occupy separate cubicles at night and congregate in a communal living space, with tables and chairs and two televisions, during the day. I conducted my research with the women housed in this facility.

In chapter 3 of this volume, I used the term *quasi-ethnography* to describe the design of my research, and I briefly discussed its commonalities with and differences from more traditional, field-based ethnography. I do not repeat that discussion here, but I do highlight the parameters of my data

---

[1] Direct-supervision facilities have several distinguishing characteristics. First, they typically entail an open style of housing, consisting of dormitory-like arrangements or individual cubicles instead of cells. Second, they usually are marked by a style of supervision that places the deputy within the housing unit itself with nothing encumbering his or her line of vision. Finally, they are supposed to have a more open style of living, with inmates freely circulating and coming and going from his or her cubicle at will.

[2] In New York State, local correctional facilities, known as penitentiaries, are county run, usually but not always under the supervision of the sheriff. They house inmates who have individual sentences of 1 year or less.

collection efforts and analytic strategies, which were consistent with the constant comparative method associated with *grounded theory,*[3] developed by Glaser and Strauss (1967) and subsequently refined by Strauss and Corbin (1998). In so doing, I address how I overcame several of the challenges involved in doing research, both qualitative and otherwise, in a jail setting.

THE DESIGN: CONSTRUCTING
LIFE HISTORIES, HUSTLING PROFILES,
AND ECOLOGIES OF SURVIVAL

As I discussed in chapter 3, I approached this study with three research interests in mind. First, I wanted to learn why my sample of chronic, low-level woman offenders had become involved in crime and immersed in a life of street hustling. Second, I sought to understand the nature of their criminal lives and the lifestyle of the hustling activities they entailed over time. Third, I wanted to gain insight into how these women survived and to chart the nature or ecology of their marginal existence on the street, its normative practices, belief structures, and institutional arrangements that enabled them to survive.

In deciding on the methods I would use to collect the up-close, information-rich data I sought, I was very much influenced by life history research conducted in the ethnographic tradition. Such an approach is in fact characteristic of contemporary scholarship on women and crime, including both pathways research and that associated with feminist thought, much of which I reviewed in chapter 2. For this reason, I decided that I would collect my data using a semistructured intensive interview schedule that would enable me to develop topical life histories of the women around the three areas of my research interests.

Before turning to a discussion of the specific qualitative strategies I used to collect and work with my data, I must stress again, as I did in chapter 3 of this volume, that this research was very much grounded in the ethnographic tradition of the early Chicago School of Sociology (Taylor

---

[3] Bachman and Schutt (2003) define *grounded theory* as "systematic theory developed inductively based on observations that are summarized into conceptual categories, reevaluated in the research setting, and gradually refined and linked to other conceptual categories" (p. I-10-11).

& Bogdan, 1998). Accordingly, what I sought to obtain with this study was what Matza (1969) called an "appreciation" of the women's "subjective view" of themselves and their worlds (p. 24). I was, as he wrote, delivered

> into the arms of the subject who renders the phenomenon, and [committed] . . . to the subject's definition of the situation . . . [with my aim being] to comprehend and to illuminate the subject's view and to interpret the world *as it appears to* [*her*]. (p. 25)

What I sought, in other words, was an "interior view" (p. 24) of the women and their lives, one that enabled me to see them with their eyes and meanings or from "the inside" so as to tell their stories "with fidelity and without violating [their] integrity" (p. 25).

OBTAINING ACCESS TO THE WOMEN

I obtained formal access to the women from the sheriff of Monroe County, who is constitutionally charged with running the county's pretrial detention (jail) facility as well as its penitentiary or local correctional facility, the MCF. *True access,* or how I entered the women's social space in the non-threatening, empathic way necessary for honest dialogue, was obtained in several ways over my initial days in the facility.

First, before any actual work began, I met and discussed the project with the two deputies posted as unit supervisors in the women's housing area. Fortunately, these women were older, more experienced deputies who had known most of the inmates, or their families, for many years. I also provided the deputies with a written script to facilitate inmate recruitment for the project. One of the deputies used this script to announce the project, after I first arrived at the jail, and it subsequently was incorporated into the orientation for each new group of admissions to the facility.

After the project was announced to the population, and during my first few days in the facility, I conducted no interviews but remained in the unit, observing and available to the inmates, to answer any questions they had and to discuss the project informally with them. A number of women sat and talked with me in the day space of the unit at different intervals over this time. Most wanted to know what "the book" was for, what its name was, and whether they would be able to buy it in the community. Some shared with me the titles of books and movies that they thought would help my research. Not much was happening in the unit in way of programming activities at this time, and many women wanted to sign up to tell me their stories. I explained the selection criteria to the women and took down the names of individuals who indicated that they met them. This was, of course, verified before any interviews were scheduled.

The housing unit deputy was instrumental in providing a measure of initial access to the population, as were my own informal interactions with the women; however, true access was possible only after the completion of several successful initial interviews or after I had established a sense of credibility and trust with the first women interviewed, which then was communicated to others in the unit. Accordingly, I was very careful in my selection of initial participants and chose several older women who appeared to have stature in the unit, thinking they would serve a possible gatekeeping function for this project (see Giallombardo, 1966; Owen, 1998). The presence, within a week of my arrival, of several women I knew also greatly facilitated my access to the population. I had met and interviewed these women 2 years ago and had a fairly good sense of rapport with them, which was sensed as they called out "hellos," followed by hugs, when they came into the unit.

At the same time, I must acknowledge that it was my daily task to maintain a presence in the housing unit that communicated to the inmates independence from the jail and its staff as well as genuine interest in them as individuals. I took great care not to overdress or to spend too much time at the deputy's station. My arrival in the unit was scheduled each day for a time after the women had risen, showered, and breakfasted. I also limited my time in the unit to the day shift (i.e., between the hours of 7:00 a.m. and 3:00 p.m.) for the convenience of the jail, its staff, and the inmates.

THE INTERVIEW SCHEDULE

The project's interview schedule consisted of open-ended questions, along with preformulated sequential probes. In addition, a number of the questions and areas examined included checklists of topics (referred to as "checkpoints") that I explored consistently with the women. The topics that these checklists comprised were suggested by the literature and a previous study (Rockell, 2004) I had conducted in this particular jail.

The schedule itself was divided into three distinct sections, each of which was intended to explore the dimensions of a particular stage in the woman's life and criminal career. The beginnings of her personal and social development was the subject of the first section, which asked the woman to describe her family and community of origin, educational achievements and aspirations, employment history, drug use patterns, and victimization history. These questions were formulated within the context of existing scholarship on typical female pathways to crime, and thus examined such matters as childhood and relational abuse, home lives, early risk-taking behaviors, and marginal educational and employment experiences.

The second section of the schedule focused on who the woman had been and currently was as an offender. The nature and volume of her arrest history were explored, and she was asked to comment on the patterns of her criminal involvement in terms of its diversity or specialization, changes over time, and periods of desistance. Also included in this section were questions relating to the woman's previous jail stays, from the earliest stay to the present one, to assess both the frequency of their occurrence and the woman's sense of their overall meaning and place in her life. As with the other parts of the interview schedule, this second section of questions relating to the woman's criminal and jail history were informed by the literature, especially that pertaining to developmental criminology and desistance (e.g., see Maruna, 2001). A major interest of the research was to secure detailed reflections by the women about how repeated jail stays had affected their lives, economically and personally, as well as their criminal careers.

There were three additional subparts to this second section of the interview schedule that were intended to yield much greater detail about the woman's criminal activity. The first subpart included questions for women who reported involvement in prostitution, either currently or in the past, and the second and third targeted women who similarly reported property offenses and drug activity, respectively. Depending on how the woman described her criminal activity(ies), she was asked questions from one, two, or all three of these subsections. The actual dynamics of her day-to-day life while criminally involved were explored, as were her impressions of the current and past social and criminal world of which she was or had been a part. The third section of the interview schedule focused on how the woman survived while outside of jail. It also included several questions that elicited her impressions about how to survive while in jail or "how to do jail" itself. With its emphasis on existence and its imagery of the woman as a survivor, this final section of the interview was unlike the others in that it explored the true assets and resources of the woman and her community or social world, while both on the street and in the jail.

In exploring the women's outside survival, I questioned each person about the people, places, and arrangements she had used or made over time to live or obtain shelter and subsistence. Periods of homelessness or times spent on the street also were discussed within the same context of assessing the means and arrangements used or made to survive. Of particular interest was the role that relationships with others had on these arrangements, as well as the woman's offending behavior. By *others* I meant family, friends, associates, dates, partners, businesses, churches, and governmental or service agencies. Also, my interest was in exploring how these others had affected the nature, patterns, and extent of survival and offending arrangements over the woman's life span.

Underlying this interest was my intent to chart and understand what might be termed the *social ecology* of each woman's survival. As a group, these women, who are frequently referred to as "marginalized," existed within similarly marginalized areas of Rochester, where the primary employment opportunities available were in hustling through the sale of drugs, boosting, or the marketing of one's body. A principal focus of this study was how the women had survived in such marginalized areas, the niches they created, and the opportunities they exploited in both the legitimate and the illegitimate worlds of their neighborhoods.

At the same time, I also asked the women about their survival in jail, when they were in effect off the street but still so very close to it. In doing this, I sought each individual's reflections about jail life, its easiest and hardest aspects, and explored its connection to the street in terms of the attitudes, norms, and characteristics first described by Irwin (1975, pp. 85–100). In particular, I examined the ways in which survival in the jail, or "jailing," as inmates referred to it, was an extension or reflection of one's marginal existence on the street, requiring the same resourcefulness and "rabble mentality" of wariness, opportunism, exploitation, and improvisation.

The interview schedule was pretested through a pilot study with a representative, socially demographic diverse group of four inmates recommended by staff for their truthfulness, as well as experienced jail staff themselves. Several revisions were made as a result of this pilot study. The length of time spent on each interview also was found to exceed what I initially expected. I had thought that an interview would not go beyond 2 hours; however, each of these trial interviews lasted between 3 and 4 hours and, as the Sheriff had not allowed the use of tape recording devices, I limited myself to one or two interviews per day. Because I usually spent at least 6 to 8 hours in the unit each day, there was a side benefit to limiting my number of interviews with the time I spent just interacting with the women, as they watched television, played cards, wrote letters, or sat in the day space area.

SAMPLE SELECTION

To recruit participants for the study, I decided to use a purposive sampling design, also called a *purposeful* or *judgment sampling design* (Bachman & Schutt, 2003; Patton, 2002). I used this selection process so I could target individuals who were "information rich and illuminative [offering] useful manifestations of the phenomenon of interest" (Patton, 2002, p. 40), which in the context of this study was a life or career of petty, street-level criminality. Included in the sample, in other words, would be women who met what was assumed to be the "typical case" (Patton, 2002, p. 236) profile of the chronic, low-level woman offender, women with multiple arrests and jail commitments for misdemeanor offenses against property and public order.

Given the focus of the research, I set as criteria for inclusion in the sample three factors: (a) recidivist status of the woman or the number of times she had been incarcerated; (b) offense type, meaning prior jail commitments for low-level property, drug, and public order convictions; and (c) the absence of prison commitments in the woman's history. The numeric cutoff as to recidivist status or what constituted a career pattern was determined with reference to prior literature and based on the data. Maruna (2001) spoke to his difficulty in operationalizing this concept of a "career criminal" in his study of criminal desistance and settled on the simple definition of the career criminal as someone "who commits a lot of crime over a span of several years" (p. 46), because he found that "every person [in his sample] offended on at least a weekly basis for some stretch of at least two years" (p. 46).

On the basis of my review of the data, discussions with the women, and subsequent observations of previously interviewed women returning to the facility within 1 or 2 weeks of release, I found that this population likewise consisted mainly of women who were frequent offenders or "old-timers," a common expression among both inmates and deputies. In fact, during the interviews, when I asked the women how many times they had been in the jail, the typical response was laughter; "a gazillion"; or a deep sigh and puzzled look, followed by "I have no idea—at least every month." However, for the purpose of this study, the numeric cutoff for inclusion was at least five incarcerations in the county jail. At most, there were only 10 women at any given time who were excluded from the sample because they were "first-timers" or had been to jail fewer than five times.

Because of the purpose and security level of the facility, offense type also did not result in the exclusion of women from the study. Almost all of the women sentenced to the facility were there because of property, public order, and drug offenses. Although I initially had thought that I would exclude from the sample women who had crimes against persons, I did not do this because a large number of women incarcerated for offenses such as simple assault, harassment, and resisting arrest had criminal histories that primarily consisted of nonviolent, property, or drug crimes.

Only two women were excluded from the study because of prior prison time. One was an African American woman in her early 40s, who reported some 30 arrests, most of which were for larcenies, and had been to prison three times for forgery offenses. Heavily involved in heroin and HIV positive, she was in jail this time for another larceny offense. The other was a 47-year-old Caucasian woman who likewise reported a history of some 25 larcenies but also had served 4 years in prison for an armed robbery. She now was back in jail for 9 months on a petty larceny charge.

On my 1st day in the facility, I obtained a printout of all women sentenced to the MCF. This printout provided both the inmates' identification numbers and the dates of their release, inclusive of *good time* (i.e., what a release date is after earned time for good behavior is subtracted from the sentence originally imposed). Using identification numbers, I then accessed the women's criminal histories, or "rap sheets," to determine the number of previous times they had been committed to the facility and the nature of their offense histories. At the end of each week of data collection, this process was done again for the women who had been committed to MCF that week.

On the basis of these checks, I compiled the names of women who satisfied the study's selection criteria. If these individuals had not approached me previously about taking part in the research, I went and spoke to them. I had to do this only five times during the project, and on only one occasion, which I discuss later in this chapter, did a woman initially not want to be interviewed.

All interviews were scheduled on the basis of the inmates' release dates, with those having earlier out-dates talked to first. In determining the sample size for the research or the time frame for my sampling, I decided that I would be guided by the two tests of "completeness," whereby one (a) has an "overall sense of meaning" and (b) reaches the point of "saturation," when nothing new is learned (Bachman & Schutt, 2003, p. 108). Although I spoke with 60 women during the time I was in the facility, completeness and saturation were in fact achieved after the first 40 interviews.

As stated, the final sample consisted of 60 women. Also, as hoped, I interviewed the entire population of women incarcerated at the time of the study who met the specific criteria for inclusion. Only 1 inmate, a 30-year-old African American who had a long history of larceny and prostitution arrests, at first did not want to participate in the study. She was released 1 week after I had begun the project; when she returned on a prostitution commitment 3 weeks later, the woman expressed her interest in participating in the research, stating that her prior disinterest had been due to the short length of time she had left on the previous sentence and that she "just didn't want to get into it."

THE INTERVIEW PROCESS

By electing to conduct this research in the jail, a setting that is coercive in nature and where everyone knows everyone else's business, it was necessary to ensure complete privacy and the lack of any sound or visual interruptions during the interview process. Most interviews were conducted in the isolation area within the female housing unit, referred to by staff and inmates as a "corridor cell" (see preface). Of all areas available for interview purposes within the facility, this was preferred for its privacy as well as its size, which facilitated a comfortable, face-to-face discussion over a small table. When the isolation area was not available because it was occupied, which happened on only two occasions, interviews took place in the laundry room.

All interviews began with a personal introduction and briefing about the project (Kvale, 1996). I explained who I was and what I was doing and why. The voluntary nature and confidentiality of the interview were explained, as were possible risks and benefits associated with the woman's involvement. I ended this briefing by telling the woman how long the interview would last and asking her, again, if she wanted to continue with it. Interviews were "framed," as suggested by Kvale (1996), and just as they opened with a briefing, where information was provided about the project, they also closed with a debriefing, where each woman was asked for any final remarks or observations.

Establishing rapport with each woman was critical to having her feel comfortable enough to exchange truthful and personally difficult information and feelings about herself and her situation. Taylor and Bogdan (1998) defined *rapport* in an action sense, focusing on what an interviewer does to achieve this state of comfort and trust or to be seen as an "okay person." They suggested that establishing a sense of rapport entails communicating empathy that is accepted as sincere by the informant; penetrating defenses against the outsider; "having people open up about their feelings . . . ; breaking through the fronts people impose in everyday life;

and sharing in informants' symbolic world, their language, and their perspectives" (p. 48).

Taylor and Bogdan (1998) also offered some general guidelines for establishing rapport, including paying homage to a person's routines, establishing what you have in common with the person, helping the person out, being humble, and acting interested (pp. 48–51). I kept these suggestions in mind, and they directed the conduct of the interviews, as did the need for empathic listening and the creation of a nonthreatening presence both during discussions and throughout my stay in MCF.

At the beginning of each interview, I broke the ice with the women by asking them standard demographic questions. Throughout each session, I remained as nonjudgmental as possible, letting the woman talk while relating interest and, at times, sympathetic understanding to what was being said (Taylor & Bogdan, 1998, pp. 99–101). Such measures facilitated not only a comfortable discussion with the women but also a process that I believe yielded honest, truthful, or valid data. Follow-up discussions were conducted as necessary to clarify something said at an initial interview or to pursue a line of questioning suggested by subsequent discussions.

ANALYTIC PROCEDURES

I used procedures commonly connected with field research (see Emerson, 1988) to work with my data. Specifically, I applied the constant comparative method associated with grounded theory developed by Glaser and Strauss (1967) and subsequently refined by Strauss and Corbin (1998). Using this method in a sequential fashion, I developed three different analytic units from the data. First, I developed six typologies of the women's distinctive pathways into crime. Second, I examined these six different groups, which are listed in chapter 3 and discussed more fully in chapter 5 of this volume, for the nature and patterns of subsequent criminality, as reported by the women themselves and by referencing criminal history data obtained from the jail records system. The third unit of analysis was the process of survival described by the women as an aggregate, regardless of group identification.

I developed a life history for each woman as soon as possible after the completion of an interview. These were organized around the three content areas of the interview schedule and sought to present, in narrative form, the woman's reflections of her past history or pathways into crime, her accounts of criminal involvement, and her day-to-day life both between jail stays and while incarcerated. To the greatest degree possible, the women's own words and expressions were used to create these narratives.

In addition to life histories, I constructed three different tables to capture and highlight themes or characteristics expressed by each woman about her background, criminality, and life between jail stays: (a) the Pathways table, (b) the Criminality table, and (c) the Survival table. The Pathways table recorded personal background information considered relevant to criminal trajectories, including both structural and process factors relating to the women's families of origin and their childhood and adolescent experiences.

The Criminality table likewise represented what the women said about their offense and jail histories, from information about their first arrest (i.e., age, type, description, and explanation) to what they reported about subsequent arrests and jail commitments. Similarly, the Survival table included information about the people, places, institutions, and arrangements used by the women to survive their lives on the street between jail stays. This exercise of representing the data in tabular form or bracketing them into smaller pieces of information for each woman preceded and actually facilitated the subsequent coding processes, which I discuss later in this chapter.

As I said earlier, the analysis was directed by the constant comparative method associated with Glaser and Strauss (1967) and Strauss and Corbin (1998). Accordingly, I began with a microscopic examination of the data, which entailed a detailed and discriminate line-by-line reading and analysis of what was said by the women along with how they said it. To facilitate this initial sorting-out process, I read and reread life history narratives, highlighting structural and process factors associated with each woman's life experience, as well as themes, expressions, or issues that appeared to recur in and distinguish the data. To better visualize this information, I tabulated the data and began the process of drafting reflective memos about observations made from them.

Moving to the next phase of analysis, that of further decontextualization of the data (Cresswell, 1998), I engaged in open coding or opened up the data to "expose the thoughts, ideas, and meanings contained therein" (Strauss & Corbin, 1998, p. 102). It is during this critical process that Strauss and Corbin (1998) stated that "the data are broken down into discrete parts, closely examined, and compared for similarities and differences . . . [which] allows for fine discrimination and differentiation among categories" (p. 102). In abstracting the data in this way, the researcher is able to identify concepts or meanings that appear to distinguish particular cases as being both similar to each other and comparatively different from all others. For instance, in examining what the women in this study expressed as their motivations for crime, several initial categories or types emerged from the data. These categories were labeled using the words of the respondents themselves or consisted of in vivo codes, because they were repeatedly spoken and at a level of description that I could not match (p. 105). Three examples of these categories were women who said they stole because (a) it was all about the money (subsequently labeled the "Show Me the Money" group) or (b) because it was something everyone in their family did (subsequently labeled the "All in the Family" group); or because (c) they experienced a thrill or "high" of getting something for nothing (subsequently labeled the "Just Another Addiction" group). Excerpts from descriptive memos that were drafted about several women representative of each group follow, in the order just specified.

Show Me the Money

Shasta said she started stealing money from her mother as a child because "I likes money." A 10th-grade dropout, Shasta told me she began to steal outside the home and get arrested "every month or so" because "I lacked a lot of things coming up. I always saw other kids with things I wanted and couldn't have." Likewise, Sherry described her childhood home as "rough, very ghetto," and said she didn't have the best of things—that she had what "I needed, but not what I wanted." Her mother, who used cocaine, which Sherry said she would never do, did the "best she could and never sold their stuff." "I like money," she said, "and gotta make it in a different way." Tracey explained her early thefts as a product of "wanting money and wanting it fast." "I got selfish in my teenage years," she said. "I like money.

I want a pair of 'Timbs' [Timberland boots]. I want my kids to have every-thing—you should see all the stuff they got from this last credit card thing."

All in the Family

Pat said she had been stealing since she was a little kid and that "everyone on [her] father's side was either a booster or a pimp." She heard stories about what her aunts and uncles did as she was growing up and, and then she saw all of her cousins boosting. Likewise, Kate described a family that was "very good at gambling and hustling," as did Esther, who said "[My] grandfather was a bookie. He taught me how to write numbers out and took me to the clubs and pool halls to pick up numbers."

Just Another Addiction

Susan laughed and told me that she had had close to 60 petty larcenies since she began to steal in her early 20s. She explained her first offense, which she committed alone, by saying, "It was a high, alright . . . I gotsta try this again!" Janie, similarly, described her booster days as "beautiful," and Cathy, when asked why she boosted, replied, "It was exciting, a high in itself. The getting and finding ways of getting. Looking, feeling good, knowing where I'm going and what I'm going for."

Initial or tentative in vivo codes for women who subsequently were grouped together in the Show Me the Money group included the follow-ing: "healthy but unwealthy," "likes money," "only the best for my kids," "wants fast money," "just can't work around money," "we all like a good buy," "don't wanna be dependent on no one," "wanna see my money," "likes nice things," and "won't go for cheap shit." Among the initial codes for women in the All in the Family group were the following: "all my aunts and uncles were boosters or pimps," "comes from a drug family," "doin' what I know," "hustlin's all I know," "of the streets," "hustlin' family," "my family's my trigger," and "it's like the family business." For women who were grouped in the Just Another Addiction group, in vivo codes were as follows: "stealin's just another high"; "I wants excitement"; "going to the block is more exciting than the clubs"; "even if I have money, I steal";

"it's like a rush"; "I get pumped up"; "I'm just a kleptomaniac"; and "my pimps's my pockets."

The preceding codes were used for an initial organization or sorting of the data, which I did manually, without the benefit of computer software. A code list was developed, and excerpts from the life histories and interviews, labeled with pseudonyms used to identify the women, were categorized accordingly.

This step of open coding or conceptualizing the data enables the researcher to reduce large amounts of data to smaller, more manageable pieces of information. At the same time, however, the act of labeling or coding in and of itself does not really lead to discovery or "any greater understanding of the what the concepts stand for or mean" (Strauss & Corbin, 1998, p. 109); what is necessary to gain this meaning or understanding is "more of the detailed, discriminate type of analysis that [Strauss and Corbin] call microanalysis" (Strauss & Corbin, 1998, p. 109). This involves the process of developing the "category in terms of its specific properties and dimensions" (Strauss & Corbin, 1998, p. 116), which in turn proceeds to the next analytical step of axial coding.

Strauss and Corbin (1998) stated that axial coding, in a procedural sense, is the "act of relating categories to subcategories along the lines of their properties and dimensions": The phenomenon, in a sense, is contextualized or "located . . . within a conditional structure [that identifies the] how or means through which a category is manifested" (p. 127). More specifically and understandably, this conditional structure involves the researcher in "answering the questions of who, when, where, why, how and with what consequences" and enables him to "relate structure with process" (p. 127). Strauss and Corbin explained the importance of this analytic activity for understanding in the following way:

> Why would one want to relate structure with process? Because structure or conditions set the stage, that is, create the circumstances in which problems, issues, happenings, or events pertaining to a phenomenon are situated or arise. Process, on the other had, denotes the action/interaction over time of persons, organizations, and communities in response to certain problems and issues. Combining structure with process helps analysts to get at some of the complexity that is so

much a part of life. Process and structure are inextricably linked, and unless one understands the nature of their relationship (both to each other and to the phenomenon in question), it is difficult to truly grasp what is going on. If one studies structure only, then one learns why but not how certain events occur. If one studies process only, then one understands how persons act/interact but not why. One must study both structure and process to capture the dynamic and evolving nature of events. (p. 127)

To demonstrate how this process was used in my study, I reference the previous examples to note how greater understanding was made of the three pathway categories by examining and distinguishing between them in terms of both structure and process. As noted, Shasta, Pat, and Susan, who were considered representative of the categories, became involved in their crime of choice, boosting, for differing reasons. Shasta said she did so because she lacked a lot of things when growing up, that although her basic needs were taken care of, she always felt healthy but unwealthy, wanting what the other kids had. In contrast, Pat stole because it was all she knew, having grown up in a family where stories about aunts and uncles who boosted or pimped were folklore told on a daily basis, and Susan did so because of being a self-proclaimed kleptomaniac who enjoyed the excitement of getting away with something for nothing. The means or processes these women used to accomplish their crimes were likewise distinct, reflective not just of the causes or reasons for their behavior but of other consequences they sought to achieve as well. These are described next, through excerpts of analytic memos written for the purpose.

Shasta told me that instead of stealing merchandise that she would then have to sell, or boost, she went for the cash, checks, or credit cards, which she has done repeatedly at the retail and waitressing jobs she has held:

At Save-A-Lot I just counted my drawer on the day I started and then put some cash in my pocket and left. At Wilson

Farms, I slipped my hand in the drop box and took money out every day I worked. And, at IHOP I left with a customer's credit card and did my Christmas shopping.

"You always try the credit cards at the closest gas station to where you grabbed them," she told me, "to make sure they're still active, and, then you run to Wal-Mart. [I just] can't work around people's money."

Pat said that when she started her thefts it was with the same cousins with whom she had stolen as a child. She also said that when it came to boosting what she had taken, it was usually to family as well. Pat's stealing continued into her clubbing years, and she says it was as much a part of that lifestyle as it was her family: "It was just a job, at first, something we all did. Then, it was like this social thing when I'd take stuff out to the clubs, flashing what I gots for everybody to see and want."

When Susan started to tell me about how she stole, she was laughing and telling me one story after another, like how she acts "obnoxious" with some store employees and "pesters" them for stuff that she knows the store does not have so that they will try to avoid her or how she one time "looked so pathetic standing in the rain with a bag of stolen stuff from K-Mart" that an employee gave her a ride home. "Guess I'm just a kleptomaniac," she said. "I gets off on boostin' and do it even when I got money in my pocket." This high also seems to extend to how Susan said she gets rid of what she has stolen. "If you're in your hospital bed and got money, I'm coming at you. If you're going into delivery, I'll sell you a bag of clothes for your baby."

In a subsequent series of memos I noted the ways in which the women differed in how they explained their initial motivations for committing crime, which in most cases were theft-related offenses or drug sales, and how the nature of their offenses seemed to reflect these underlying reasons. Shasta, for example, who had been initially characterized as someone who "wants fast money," was seen as being just about the money: She wanted nothing between her and it, be it time or additional effort. Accordingly, she seemed to use jobs where she had direct access to cash or credit to steal. In contrast, Susan, who was coded in the category of "wants the excitement" of boosting, was all about the challenges and euphoric feelings experienced when stealing something and getting paid for it, deriving a sense of competency or a high because she had "gotten over" or outhustled somebody. In a sense, boosting was who Susan was, and it gave her a feeling not dissimilar to a drug-induced euphoria. Pat, however, who had been coded as in the category of "doing what I know," said stealing was something she learned and began as a child, having grown up in a family steeped in deviance with lifestyles that sustained it. Stealing was like a job or the family business, in a sense, and she worked with family members both to accomplish theft and to unload what she had stolen.

Another concept or category that was axial coded or contextualized in this fashion was a word that I heard throughout the study, and that was *lick* (see chap. 1). This term was used by nearly every woman I interviewed, from those in jail for prostitution to those serving time for theft or drug-related offenses. After several interviews, which included direct questioning of the women about the meaning of the term to them, I realized that what they were referring to by this concept of "the lick" was the criminal event that they pursued or how they were able to lick (i.e., beat, trick, or scam) someone or something out of money, merchandise, or some other valued commodity, such as drugs, through crime. To a person, the women indicated that on a typical day when they were criminally active their main objective was to "catch a lick," and their dream was that it be a "good lick."

As implied previously, the nature or substance of the lick varied on the basis of what a person primarily did in terms of crime. However, among women within each offense category (i.e., prostitution, theft-related crimes, and drug offenses) there was uniform agreement as to the who, what, where, when, and how that was necessary for one to achieve a good lick or the ideal situation for a particular crime. These included both personal attributes associated with cunning, skill, and decision making, as well as more situational elements related to good versus bad targets, time of day, locations, and customers.

As a final analytic procedure or to recontextualize the data (Cresswell, 1998), I also engaged in coding for process, using what Strauss and Corbin (1998) called the "conditional/consequential matrix." This coding device was used to reflect on and to determine from the data the "relationships between macro and micro conditions and consequences both to each other and to process" (p. 181). What I did, in other words, was to posit in memorandum form the macro- and microconditions and consequences that emerged from the data and the ways in which they intersected and interacted to become a part of the situational context of the phenomena being examined. I used this procedure to delineate, understand, and distinguish differing pathways into crime and the women's offending patterns as well as the strategies they used for survival discussed in the chapters that follow.

As I stated at the outset of this chapter, I applied the analytic procedures detailed earlier to three different units in the study. First, I examined the narrative or life histories of the women to identify six analytically distinct trajectories into crime (see chaps. 3 and 5). Second, I developed the criminal histories of these six groups, compiled from information supplied by the women as well as the jail criminal history database, to assess whether patterns of activity existed within each group and distinguished one group from another. The third and final unit of analysis was the process of survival engaged in by women who said they lived on the street between jail stays, irrespective of group membership or criminal activity.

CONCLUDING REMARKS

I have presented in this chapter a rather thorough discussion of my research design and analytic strategies. Given the nature and location of the study, I have placed special emphasis on activities related to gatekeeping, rapport building, and confidentiality. Issues relating to questions of generalizability, validity, and reliability also were addressed and may be learned by contacting me directly at St. John Fisher College in Rochester,

New York. The results of my endeavor are presented in the next three chapters, beginning with the next one, chapter 5, in which I describe the physical and social environment of the city where most of the women grew up and lived. Also included in chapter 5 is a discussion of the six pathways to crime that characterized the women's initial entry and involvement in criminality.

PART TWO

PEOPLE, PATTERNS, PLACES

5

The Women's Physical Environment, Social Milieu, and Pathways to the Street

Reviewers have said that this is the most sobering chapter of the book and that the stories told in it are quite sad and painful. Indeed they are, and the women themselves often seemed reluctant "to go there" or to spend any great amount of time recalling their pasts. In fact, they made repeated remarks about how these memories were "just that" and not all there was to them. Although I certainly expected them to, and would not have faulted them for doing so, most also did not see themselves as hapless victims; neither did they dwell on the pain of their pasts, opting instead to talk about their wits, skills, and adventures "back in the day" when hustling was fun, a high, or just the way it was and they were in the earliest stages of addiction. One might be tempted, I suppose, to call them "resourceful survivors," both of their pasts and the streets, and many did in fact see themselves as such back in that same day; unfortunately, however, that label now clearly seems an ironic misnomer, because most of these women have been irreparably harmed by the hustling and drug-involved lifestyle they once lived. I sincerely hope that readers are able to see the many contours, and not just the sadness, of these women in this chapter and those that follow.

ROCHESTER, NEW YORK: THE WOMEN'S CITY OF ORIGIN AND RESIDENCE

With 6 exceptions, the childhood neighborhoods of the 60 women interviewed for this study were located in marginal and working class areas of the city of Rochester, New York. The six who did not grow up in these areas fared little better in their early lives spent on the Tonawanda Reservation and in rural towns to the west of the city.

The city of Rochester is typically represented as consisting of four geographical quadrants, branching from its center, with each bordered by the Genesee River and Lake Ontario toward the north. The 54 city residents were fairly evenly distributed among three of these quadrants: (a) the northwest quadrant, where 19 women had been raised as children; (b) the southwest quadrant, which had been the residence of another 17; and (c) the northeast quadrant, where 18 had lived. The specific neighborhoods in which they were raised are today collectively called the *Crescent District*, or *the Crescent*, because they form an arc around the city center.

The Crescent, which seems to make daily headlines in Rochester, is known for much more than its shape. It has been the site of the majority of the city's record-level homicides, as well as its other social and economic ills stemming from an increasing concentration of poverty and residential patterns fueled by race and class divisiveness. In 2004, for instance, it was in this area, where less than 27% of Rochester's population resides, that approximately 80% of its murders occurred (Klofas, 2004).

In many respects, Rochester and Monroe County, within which it is located, represent extremely different economic and social worlds for residents living either within city limits or in the 30 towns and villages of the county. This is evident from just a cursory look at U.S. census data for 2004 (U.S. Census Bureau, 2004), which is summarized in the paragraphs that follow.

Monroe County, with Lake Ontario as its northern border, encompasses 659 square miles, 36 of which consist of Rochester itself. Some 735,343 people reside in the county, an increase of 3% over the 1990 numbers, and nearly 80% of these residents are Caucasian. The county compares well with the state in terms of economic and education data. The median county household income is nearly $45,000, in contrast to the state median of just over $43,000; the home ownership rate is over 65%, compared with 53% for the state, with a median value for county structures in excess of $98,000. Also, the county poverty rate in 1999 was 11.2% compared with the state rate of 14.6%. Regarding education, the county boasts a population of 84.9% high school graduates and over 31% residents with baccalaureate degrees, compared with the state rates of 79% and 27%, respectively (U.S. Census Bureau, 2004).

A contrasting picture emerges in the county seat of Rochester. The population there is just over 200,000, down nearly 5% since 1990. Its population is 51.7% minority, with the two largest groups being African American (38.5%) and Hispanic (12.8%). The median income is just over $27,000; home ownership is 40%, with a median home value of $61,300. The city's poverty rate is about 26%, nearly double that for the state. Also below state rates are educational indicators: Seventy-three percent of city residents are high school graduates, and 20% hold baccalaureate degrees or higher (U.S. Census Bureau, 2004).

For many people in Monroe County, the declining city of Rochester has been seen "as simply a hole in the middle of an otherwise healthy donut" (Metropolitan Forum, 1996, p. 4). Although the city population has steadily declined since its peak year in 1950, the population of the county's 20 towns and 10 villages has swelled by over 250,000. Also, the city's ethnic makeup is now predominantly minority—a big change from a racial makeup of 97.7% Caucasian in 1950. The profound implications of these population changes go beyond mere census data, however.

The role of Rochester in the community life of the county mirrors what has happened in many other U.S. cities. The city's economic base has changed from manufacturing and industrial to financial, information, and service industries, which require higher levels of education than jobs of the past, and even this new economic base has left for the suburbs. Transitioning from an urban center to a metropolitan community, the growing regionalism in the area has transformed "economic life, transportation, entertainment, social life—nearly all aspects of life" (Metropolitan Forum, 1996, p. 2).

The result for Rochester has been a growing concentration of poverty, accompanied by all ancillary social and economic indicators. Although the county itself has experienced a mere 1% increase in its rate of poverty over the past 25 years, the city has seen more than a doubling of its poverty rate, rising from 12% to 25% in the past 20 years (Metropolitan Forum, 1996). Moreover, when looking at the county and the city of Rochester in both geographical and racial terms, it is clear that Monroe County is a highly segregated area. All but 1 of the 49 census tracts designated as poverty tracts (i.e., where 20% or more of the people live below the poverty level) are located in the city, and all 15 census tracts of extreme poverty (i.e., where 40% or more of the people live below the poverty level) are within city limits. When one adds race to this picture, the distribution of poverty is clearly disproportionate in the area: Only 7% of the county's Caucasian residents are poor, compared with 32% of its African American residents and 36% of its Hispanic residents (Metropolitan Forum, 1996).

Combining race and geography provides an even clearer picture of how concentrated poverty is in Monroe County. Although the city population of Rochester is predominantly minority, there is only one suburban town where that population exceeds 4%. This shows, then, that whereas

> 40% of poor Whites live in the city of Rochester, . . . 87% of poor Blacks and 91% of poor Hispanics live within city, [leading] to one of the most important facts of poverty [in the county]: three fourths of all poor Whites live in middle class neighborhoods, often in the suburbs, while 80% of poor Blacks and Hispanics live in poor neighborhoods, all of which are in the city. (Metropolitan Forum, 1996, p. 3)

This concentration of poverty in the city of Rochester, combined with a declining population, loss of middle-class families and businesses to the suburbs, and falling tax base, has created social consequences that are far greater than the overall poverty level might suggest. As the Metropolitan Forum (1996) observed,

> Physical separation from jobs and middle-class role models, and dependency on a dysfunctional welfare system reinforce isolation from the American mainstream [where individuals] are far more likely to become pregnant as teenagers, drop out of high school and remain jobless, than if they lived in socio-economically mixed neighborhoods. (p. 3)

The consequences of concentrated poverty for the city of Rochester have been well documented. Some 10 years ago, for example, the Metropolitan Forum (1996) reported the following:

[In an examination of Rochester City Schools, it was found] that the average city high school student carries a D average and is a full grade behind where he or she should be. The City schools now grant fewer [New York State] Regents' Diplomas than they did seven years ago and Rochester schools lead the state in drop-out and suspension rates. In its Child Health Report Card, the Monroe County Health Department with the University of Rochester reported rising rates of infant mortality, teen pregnancy and violence in our community. In fact, violence levels are so concentrated that the homicide risk for young African American men living in the high poverty rates is 60 times that of the rest of the community. (p. 3)

More recent data are even more troubling. First, with respect to educational data, Klofas (2003) reported that whereas the city educates 31% of all public school students in the county, they are responsible for only 12% of county high school graduates and 3% of county New York State Regents degrees. In an even more telling representation, he reported that of the freshman class entering city schools for the 1996–1997 academic year, only 26% graduated 4 years later and only 4% with Regents diplomas.

Data and reports on numerous quality of life and health indicators in the city are just as disturbing. Stating that "it's awful and embarrassing, particularly in a community with so many resources," a faculty member in the Department of Public Health Practice at the University of Rochester, in discussing infant mortality rates in certain parts of the city which are twice the national average, recently added, "It's like a third world country" (Becker, 1999, p. 2). Nearly 40% of the city's children under age 5 are living in poverty; its teen birth rate remains 3 to 4 times higher than the overall rate in central New York; less than half of its students meet state educational standards; and its number of new foster care admissions remain above the rate for New York state—excluding New York City rates (Pryor, 2003).

The existence of two very disparate social and economic worlds in Monroe County and Rochester, which was once described as Smugtown, USA (Gerling, 1957), has generated comment by many, including David Rusk, an urbanologist who visited the area in the late 1990s. In discussing the consequences of concentrated poverty in Rochester, Rusk (1994, cited in Metropolitan Forum, 1996) said the city "was fast approaching 'the point of no return' [, and given its] population loss, minority population con-centration, and income gap between the city and suburbs" (pp. 3–4), was about to join his list of failed cities.

THE WOMEN AS AN AGGREGATE

The sample of 60 women interviewed for this research included the entire population of women committed to the Monroe County Correctional Facil-ity over a 5-month period who met the criteria for inclusion in the study. The sample consisted of 32 African American women, 21 Caucasian women, 2 Hispanic women, 2 Native American women, 1 African American–Hispanic woman, 1 Caucasian–Hispanic woman, and 1 Caucasian–Native American woman (see Table 5.1). Their ages ranged from 19 to 51, with an average age of 36.4 years. Two of the women were under age 20, 11 were in their 20s, 25 were in their 30s, 19 were in their 40s, and 3 were over age 50. The average age of the African American women (35.6 years) was slightly less than that of the Caucasian women (38 years).

The majority of the women ($n = 40$) were single, never married. Ten were divorced, 5 were separated, 4 were married, and 1 was widowed. Only 4 of the women had never had a child. The 56 mothers had birthed 174 children altogether, for an average of 3.1 children per woman. Of these 56 women, just over 20% ($n = 12$) indicated that their minor child or children had lived with them before their last arrest. For the 44 women who did not live with their minor children, placements were distributed among family (e.g., grand-mothers, sisters, fathers), foster care, and adoptions. Only 2 children had been placed at birth, another 15 were incarcerated, 8 were deceased, and the locations of 5 were unknown or "on the street."

The vast majority of women ($n = 56$) had not been legally employed before their most recent incarceration. Of the few who had been working in licit jobs, employment was intermittent or temporary and generally limited to work in laundries, dry cleaners, or home health care (see Table 5.2). The rest of the women reported surviving through a combination of hustling, government assistance, under-the-table odd jobs in the neighborhood, or support by family or partners. Conventional employment histories were like-wise limited and, for some of the women, nonexistent. Most of the women

Table 5.1

Demographic Characteristics of the Women as Adults

Characteristic	%	n
Race		
African American	53.3	32
Caucasian	35.0	21
Hispanic	3.3	2
Native American	3.3	2
African American–Hispanic	1.7	1
Caucasian–Hispanic	1.7	1
Caucasian–Native American	1.7	1
Total	100.0	60
Age at time of interview (years)		
Under 20	3.3	2
20–24	6.6	4
25–29	11.7	7
30–34	16.7	10
35–39	25.0	15
40–44	16.7	10
45–49	15.0	9
50+	5.0	3
Total[a]	100.0	60
Marital status		
Single/never married	66.7	40
Married	6.7	4
Divorced	16.7	10
Separated	8.3	5
Widowed	1.7	1
Total	100.1	60
Children[b]		
0	6.7	4
1	13.3	8
2	21.7	13
3	30.0	18

(continued)

Table 5.1

Demographic Characteristics of the Women as Adults (*Continued*)

Characteristic	%	n
4	11.7	7
5	8.3	5
6	6.7	4
10	1.7	1
Total	100.1	60
Location of children before mother's arrest		
With woman	12.6	22
Woman's mother	18.4	32
Woman's sister	5.2	9
Woman's aunt	3.4	6
Woman's grandmother	5.2	9
Other family of woman	1.2	2
With father	10.3	18
Foster care	10.9	19
Adoption	7.5	13
Incarcerated	8.6	15
Street—unknown	2.9	5
Older—on own	8.0	14
Placed at birth	1.2	2
Deceased	4.6	8
Total	100.0	174

[a]Percentage totals do not exactly equal 100 because some numbers were rounded.
[b]Number of children reported by the women.

who reported past employment had worked within the service sector of Rochester, and there was 1, a college graduate, who said she had been a social worker in her past, working with adults with developmental disabilities. Ten women said they had never worked, with the exception of selling drugs.

All but 1 of the women reported an extensive personal history of alcohol and/or drug use, and 90% of them ($n = 54$) said they had been using drugs regularly before this most recent incarceration. Cocaine or crack was the drug of choice for 43, and the remaining 16 were equally distributed between

Table 5.2

Past Employment History of the Women

Employment type	%	n
None	16.7	10
SSI	10.0	6
Maintenance–cleaning	11.7	7
Fast food	10.0	6
Restaurant or bar	8.3	5
Stripping	6.7	4
Retail	10.0	6
Clerical	8.3	5
Heath field	11.7	7
Factory	5.0	3
Professional	1.7	1
Total[a]	100.1	60

Note: SSI = Supplemental Security Income.
[a]Percentage total does not exactly equal 100 because some numbers were rounded.

reporting use of heroin and marijuana and alcohol. The average age of start-ing use was 21.1 years. Current heroin users were considerably older than women who reported crack as their drug of choice: On average, the former were 41 years old, and the latter were 23.2 years old.

The women's overall health when admitted to jail was marginal at best. Only three women reported that they had no medical problems to speak of at the time of the interview. At least seven indicated a diagnosis of HIV/AIDS, and another five said they had hepatitis C. Among other physical problems reported were cancer, heart disease, diabetes, brain injuries, hypertension, lupus, aneurisms, glaucoma, arthritis, and a variety of sexually transmitted diseases. Mental health issues were numerous as well, with at least 90% of the women indicating that they were on medication for depression, anxiety, bipolar disorder, attention-deficit disorder, or posttraumatic stress disorder.

With very few exceptions, the childhood homes of the women reflected the social ills of the areas where they were located, which, as stated earlier, were in the Crescent District of the city of Rochester. Most reported disruptive family lives in which the primary constants were violence, drugs, and crime. Only 6 of the women said they had not experienced abusive child-hoods, and 52 reported that they had family members who were in jail or prison. Only a handful ($n = 8$) indicated the consistent presence of both par-ents in the home during childhood, and the majority ($n = 50$) reported alco-hol and drug involvement by either one or both of these caregivers or others who had assumed the task, most often grandparents.

The socioeconomic backgrounds of the women's families were, with very few exceptions, either marginal or working class. Racial differences were apparent in both the economic life and the well-being of the women's families. African American, Hispanic, and Native American participants reported that adult caregivers in their pasts had primarily made ends meet in the home by limited service sector employment, typically as home health aides, maintenance workers, laundry staff, or cleaning personnel, along with various forms of governmental aid. These women also indicated that their families had received charitable contributions, through churches and neighborhood organizations, and that their caregivers had engaged in both unconventional money-making activities (e.g., selling dinners, hosting card parties, gambling) as well as illicit behaviors, primarily shoplifting and selling drugs.

In contrast, Caucasian caregivers were employed in typical working class jobs. Many of these women's parents had worked in Rochester and outlying area factories, including Kodak, Delco, Rochester Products, Bausch & Lomb, Archway, Wegmans, Gleasons, Xerox, and Heinz. Several others worked in construction-related activities, drove cabs, or managed bars or restaurants. Although drug-related activity was not mentioned as a familial source of income by these women, other unconventional and illicit behaviors aimed at generating money were described by a handful. These were limited to the hosting of card or drinking parties and fencing (i.e., selling stolen goods).

The educational experiences of the women were evenly mixed: Thirty said they liked school, and 30 said they did not. The majority of women ($n = 46$) had not graduated from high school: Four left in 12th grade, 10 left in 11th grade, 17 left in 10th grade, 11 left in 9th grade, 3 left in 8th grade, and 1 left in 6th grade (see Table 5.3). The most common reason for leaving was preg-nancy ($n = 18$), followed by expulsion for "being bad" ($n = 8$) and "because

Table 5.3

Characteristics of the Women's Childhood Families

Characteristic	%	n
Presence of abuse		
Sexual abuse as child	25.0	15
Physical abuse as child	16.7	10
Emotional abuse as child	6.7	4
Sexual or physical abuse as child	20.0	12
Domestic violence in home	11.7	7
Domestic violence and sexual abuse	3.3	2
Domestic violence and physical abuse	6.7	4
No abuse reported as child	10.0	6
Total[a]	100.1	60
Parental absence		
Mother present only intermittently	5.0	3
Father present only intermittently	33.3	20
Both parents present only intermittently	3.3	2
Mother present/father out of home	23.3	14
Father present/mother out of home	1.8	1
Both parents present	13.3	8
Both parents absent/raised by others	20.0	12
Total	100.0	60
Parental drug/alcohol abuse		
Mother past drug/alcohol user	15.0	9
Father past drug/alcohol user	21.7	13
Both parents past drug/alcohol users	43.3	26
No parental drug/alcohol use	20.0	12
Total	100.0	60
Family imprisonment[b]		
Mother incarcerated	9.3	8
Father incarcerated	23.3	20
Both parents incarcerated	11.6	10
Other family members incarcerated	46.5	40
No family members incarcerated	9.3	8
Total	100.0	86

(*continued*)

Table 5.3		
Characteristics of the Women's Childhood Families (*Continued*)		
Characteristic	%	*n*
Educational background		
Left in Grade 6	1.7	1
Left in Grade 8	6.7	3
Left in Grade 9	21.7	11
Left in Grade 10	31.7	17
Left in Grade 11	25.0	10
Left in Grade 12	6.7	4
Graduated high school	6.7	4
Total	100.2	60

[a]Percentage totals do not exactly equal 100 because some numbers were rounded.
[b]Total does not equal number of women who reported familial imprisonments (*N* = 52), because several women reported multiple incarcerated family members (e.g., parents and other family members).

I was grown" (*n* = 4). One woman had earned a bachelor's degree, and another had earned an associate's degree.

THE WOMEN'S PATHWAYS TO THE STREET

As stated earlier, the primary data collection method used in this study was the life history method. After each intensive interview, I developed a life history of the woman structured around the three interests or topics of what was learned about the individual in terms of (a) background, (b) offending behavior, and (c) lifestyle while criminally active. Tables were also constructed for each of these interests to visualize the data and to facilitate the early identification of themes and characteristics among the women.

My first interest, and the subject of this chapter, was to determine whether the women evinced distinct trajectories into criminal involvement. Using analytic procedures associated with grounded theory, I uncovered what appeared to be six distinct pathways or trajectories into crime for the women.

These six pathways included the following: (a) an All in the Family group, which consisted of individuals with backgrounds and life histories steeped in deviance, for whom crime was just something everyone in their family did; (b) a Partiers by Trade group, which consisted of women who became involved in crime primarily as a result of their own fast, partying lifestyles to which they had typically run as a result of dysfunctional familial relationships; (c) a Show Me the Money group, which consisted of women of more nurturing and privileged backgrounds, who appeared to pursue crime rationally as a means to get the money and things they wanted; (d) a Challenged group, which consisted of women with multiple emotional or psychological difficulties who committed crime solely to obtain drugs for self-medicating purposes; (e) a Just Another Addiction group, which consisted of women who relished the euphoric feelings they experienced when committing crime and equated their addiction to these as more powerful than any drug; and (f) a Lives of Loss and Trauma group, which consisted of women who found in crime and criminal cohorts a sense of belonging, meaning, and family that they had been denied or that had been taken from them as a result of traumatic losses and events in their lives.

In the paragraphs that follow, I discuss the pathways and the distinguishing characteristics of each of these six groups. As I noted in chapter 2, the women's names are pseudonyms to protect the confidentiality of participants.

All in the Family: Pat, Elisa, Esther, Marie, Terri, Kate, Doris, Ann, Karla, and Angela

Everyone on my dad's side was either a booster or a pimp. I done it all, darlin'.

—Marie

The women in this group appeared on the surface to resemble the African American street women profiled by E. Miller (1986). This was especially true in terms of their trajectories into crime, which at first seemed to be explained by the nexus of their families of origin with deviant street arrangements. In other words, illegality was not only part of their family history but also normatively institutionalized within the communities where these families resided. Every one of the women reported exposure to crime in the home, through the activities of grandparents, parents, uncles, and aunts, and each had also grown up in areas where prostitution, violence, and drugs were a very visible and known part of her neighborhood.

All of the women in this category were African American. Their average age was 39.6, and all but one was single, never married. The one married woman was also the only individual in the group who had retained custody of her children, as well as those of her sister, who was in prison. None of the women had graduated from high school, and all but two had some work experience, primarily in the service or retail arena. One of the two who had never worked said that her only real job had been selling drugs, and the other said she had "worked in a carnival once, handling money which [she] never stole." Although they reported that most of their offenses were larcenies, all of these women also said that they had a few prostitution charges in their pasts, and three had recent possession charges as well.

The pasts of these women had many commonalities that, when taken together, distinguished them from women in the other five categories. Their childhoods were marked, for example, by a significant amount of residential instability or movement between people and places. Terri, whose mother had been incarcerated in a state facility, said she had moved from house to house with each of her 13 aunts until her mom's release from prison, after which she spent several years with her in New York City. Doris mentioned eight addresses her mother had on the west side of Rochester, and Esther had moved between her grandmother's and mother's different houses 10 times. Kate had lived with a variety of grandparents, aunts, and uncles, as had Marie, and Elisa said she "bounced back and forth between [her] mother's and grandmother's" and also had spent "8 years in and out of lock-ups" (which consisted mainly of juvenile detention facilities in upstate New York and the Albany area). Regardless of with whom they lived, the areas where these women grew up were said to be "wild and exciting, full of violence and drugs."

The women also shared a very deep and diverse family history of criminal involvement. Terri's mother did time for homicide, and many of her aunts engaged in prostitution and sold drugs, which Terri said she saw them prepare in their kitchens. Marie also provided a list of relatives who were currently or had been in prison, and Elisa said that "back in the day [her] mom was wild with cocaine"; she also said that she knew of three men who could be her father. Pat, whose father was killed when she was 10, said that she "saw everyone in [her] family boosting or pimping" and that she "loved to hear the stories of what they'd done." Esther talked of her grandfather, who was a bookie and introduced her to hustling; he also used to beat her grandmother, and the two of them "cut each other" on occasion. Kate's grandparents liked to gamble, and there were always card games going in their basement;, it was from her grandmother, she said, that she learned about prostitution. Doris loved her family but said she had to do so from a distance because they were her "big trigger, gettin' high, drinkin', and prostitutin'."

The families of these women not only exposed them all to crime but also played a critical role in getting them started and sustaining their initial criminal involvements. Pat boosted with cousins and sold what she stole to family. Esther learned how to write numbers out (i.e., place gambling bets) from her grandfather and went to the pool halls with him to pick up numbers (for bets to be placed). Kate also learned to hustle from her grandfather, and when she started stealing she used his connections on the streets to boost merchandise.

Terri first did drugs with her aunts, who would give her "woolies" (i.e., cigars with the tobacco removed and replaced by marijuana and cocaine); she also learned how to prostitute from them, seeing dates coming and going from their houses, as well as sitting in the back seats of cars where they were working. It was, she said, when she was 13 or 14 that she was first pimped, by one of her aunts. Marie traced her penchant for drinking and fighting back to her mother's house, where there were "loud and wild" parties every weekend. She also said her "uncle was a pimp, both brothers were pimps, and I almost pimped." Doris likewise began her partying with family, starting at 12 with a mother who made her boilermakers (i.e., a shot of whiskey followed by a beer chaser) and progressing to sniffing and freebasing cocaine with sisters and aunts when she was a young adult. According to Elisa, it was not until she was around her cousins that she began to steal, when they told her "I know how to get your own. It's easy."

Although when reminiscing about their families, these women used such words as *fun, exciting, wild, busy, curious, noisy,* and *bittersweet,* they became much more solemn when asked for memories and descriptions of their childhood and family life growing up. In fact, to a person, they seemed to have experienced lost childhoods, and in general said they did not have one, or that they had gone from being a child to an adult at a very young age. When asked to describe her childhood, Terri responded as all of the women did: "I didn't have a childhood. I'm 39, and I feel like a teenager."

Most of these women reported that they were the teenage caregivers of younger brothers or sisters. "I was like Ma," Angela said, whose crack-using mother put her and her two much younger brothers out of the house at 4:00 a.m. when Angela was 14 years old. In recalling the one Christmas gift she had received from her mother, Angela asked, "Do you remember the 'Where's the beef?' puzzle that you got at Burger King, I think?" Doris, who had her first baby at age 13 and her second at age 17, said she went from a child to an adult when she left school in 10th grade to care for five younger sisters and a brother after her mother's hospitalization with the delirium tremens. She said she lied about her age to get a job, recounting where she went in downtown Rochester to obtain a fake ID and a wig to look older. I heard the same from five other women in the group who all began working in local neighborhood businesses by age 13 or 14.

For several of the women, it was not they who were caregivers, but older siblings who watched out for them as well as for other younger brothers and sisters. The quality of this care was marginal at best. Karla was the only girl in a family of nine brothers, with a mother and father who used cocaine and "couldn't be in the house for 5 seconds without arguing." Although "no one messed with [her] because of [these] brothers," she remembered them "always being in trouble" and "going to visit one or another in jail" when she was a small child. Esther's older brother took care of her; "He was into all kinds of drugs" and introduced her to crack, becoming her dealer and cheating her on sales when she was 17. A "300-pounder," the brother "wanted to make [Esther] tough"; at the time of this study, he was in prison, serving 25 years to life for murder.

All but one of the women reported leaving school by age 15, on average because of a pregnancy. All also said they had experienced either childhood sexual abuse or an adolescent rape. Six of the 10 said that it was because of this victimization that they no longer trusted men, "didn't mess with them," and preferred women as their sexual partners.

Partiers by Trade: Tess, Jenna, Linda, Jess, Kristen, Shawna, Inga, Donna, Missy, Elise

> I always worked guys on the side, whether waitressing or dancing:
> There's lots of easy slays out there.
>
> —Jess

The Partiers by Trade pathway included women who initially became involved in crime and hustling through the lifestyles of the jobs they held, which generally progressed from waitressing and bartending to dancing and stripping. At the time of this study, these 10 women were in jail on prostitution charges; however, their offense histories included a variety of offenses, ranging from larcenies and forgeries to the ancillary charges associated with their present lifestyle of disorderly conduct and loitering. All of these women came from working class backgrounds, had very poor or no relationships with their mothers, had few or no aspirations as adolescents, began working early in their lives, and self-proclaimed themselves as "always being a little wild." Eight of the 10 were Caucasian, and 2 were Native American. Their average age was 40.2 years; 3 of them had been married but were now divorced or separated. All were mothers and, with 1 exception, all had lost custody of their children years back in what was typically a very troubled, drug-involved past.

It is this past that is of interest here, because it distinguishes the pathways of these women to their present lifestyle from other categories in the study and justifies their grouping in this category. Some very common themes are apparent; several of them were highlighted earlier in this chapter when I described the six pathways. Primary among them is a confused or absent relationship with their mothers very early in life.

Tess, for instance, said her mother, a stay-at-home mom, "never told [her] that she loved [her], that she had no self or feelings," personality traits that Tess attributed to both her mom's alcoholism and her Irish heritage. Donna, who as a child in 1957 saw her 5-year-old brother killed by a bus, said she had "a lotta those years blacked out" but remembered how her mother dealt with her and a younger sister afterward using "tough love and Manhattans." The mothers of Jenna, Inga, Kristen, and Linda also were alcoholics who were either physically absent from the house most days and nights or emotionally detached, with "frequent mad parties" and a succession of dates, which often included or led to loud verbal and physical altercations in the home. Jess recalled how she "often walked in on [her] mom cheating on [her] father" and Shawna, when describing her childhood, used the word *different,* saying that her "mom was not ready to be a mother. She had a nervous breakdown when my sister was born and initially gave her up, but then reclaimed her."

Relationships with fathers also were complicated for these women. When she first responded to the question asking her to describe her childhood neighborhood, Tess said, "fine, normal, little kids growing up in an apartment complex;" in contrast, 15 minutes later, when asked to talk about her family growing up, she became far more open, saying it was

> dysfunctional, not good at all. My mother was in her place, usually "out there" [i.e., intoxicated] by five and my dad—it was like walking on eggshells. One minute he loved me to death and the next he was screamin'. Just never knew if he was gonna go off when drinkin'.

Kristen likewise initially described her childhood as "Disneyland—it keeps me going. Easter baskets, the Cleavers. I was very lazy and spoiled, the last of nine." She later recalled "Dad was never there, he always worked or just stayed away. We had two different generations of kids in the house and there was always someone else there besides us." Her father eventually moved out of state after retiring when Kristen was 14, and she has not seen him since.

All of the women in this group reported that their fathers, like most of the mothers, were drinkers or alcoholics. The women were evenly split in how they characterized their relationship with their fathers: Half said their fathers were always working, on trips, or never around, and half reported being "spoiled rotten" when their fathers were in their lives. All had witnessed their parents' divorce, usually after a marriage marked by much violence or many extramarital affairs, but most said that everything that went on in their homes happened "behind closed doors." Four of the women subsequently grew up with their fathers, and 6 grew up with their mothers. These stepfamilies were of little improvement over the women's families of origin. They, too, were "loud and argumentative," with a great deal of fighting between the parents, usually fueled by alcohol. Eight of the 10 women reported the early deaths of either their birth fathers or mothers.

Although nearly half of the women in this group graduated from high school, and all had an extensive early work history, they, more so than other women in the study, had very few aspirations for themselves during childhood. When asked what they wanted to be when they grew up, the most frequent responses were "You know what? I don't know. A mom and wife?"; "I didn't think about it"; "I didn't have any idea"; "I had no goals. I survived"; "Nobody talked about it. I didn't know college existed"; or, as Tess cryptically said, "Who knows—but not a drug addict, that's for sure." For the two women who did recall aspirations, Linda and Shawna, the former wanted to be "like Jacques Cousteau" and the latter a "soap opera actress," somewhat unrealistic goals garnered from the fantasy of television.

School was generally boring to these women, even for those who graduated. They preferred "hanging out in the city," "getting high," or "running the streets." For those who did not complete their education, leaving was not occasioned by a pregnancy or expulsion. Instead, they left, generally in the 10th grade, solely because, as Kristen said, "I could."

All of these women also began their partying, hanging out at the bars, or running the streets at a very young age, on average by the time they were 15 years old. Within, or perhaps because of these venues they generally began using drugs earlier than the other women and progressed quickly from alcohol, typically their first drug, to their current drug of choice, which was either cocaine or heroin. This span of time was no more than a few years, with all of the partiers indicating their first use of either crack or heroin by their late teens or early 20s. All of the Partiers by Trade women were on their own by the time they were 17 years old. Half of them had run away from home by that time, and the other half had married, with spouses met through the partying lifestyle.

Unlike women in other groups, these women reported more incidents of emotional and physical abuse as children than sexual abuse, with only one, Inga, saying that her father raped her at age 10, in response to which she ran to her sister's house, saying, "I wasn't goin' for that." However, much more so than others, these individuals experienced extensive sexual and physical battery in relationships they entered during late adolescence and early adulthood. All reported rapes and some measure of physical abuse by boyfriends or ex-husbands. Jess, who left her ex-husband because she "got bored," said her current boyfriend, with whom she has a child now in his custody, "hunts [her] down every night in the city, [telling dates she has AIDS], and slapping [her] around." Tess, whom I had met in a previous study last year, presented a more extreme case of victimization, as did Shawna.

Everyone in the unit, both inmates and staff, knew Tess, and they all talked about her changed and changing appearance due to the beatings she had sustained and continued to receive from her current partner, one of the few named pimps by the women. She referred to herself as "Elephant Lady" during the interview, pointing to the swelling and discoloration under her eyes and bumps and bald spots on her head. Tess said she had "vertigo—from him beating me in the head too many times" and told me a story that many in the unit knew and kept repeating to her, trying to convince her to finally leave the situation. "He told me where he dug my grave," Tess said, "and he took me there last month. He did a hit of crack and wanted his dick sucked. That's what saved me."

Shawna likewise had suffered numerous beatings from her "male friend." "He broke my ankle in half with a baseball bat," she said, "and threw me outside in my underwear." Another beat and raped her at knifepoint, joined by his best friend. Her most recent "friend beat [her] with a golf club and tried to strangle [her]," after which she "went crazy and got locked up in R-Wing [i.e., the psychiatric observation ward at Rochester's Strong Memorial Hospital] for a month."

The partying lifestyle also influenced the career choices made by the women and their behaviors while so engaged. As stated earlier, all of these women waitressed, tended bar, danced, and stripped during early adulthood, and their hustling typically began while so employed. Jess, for instance, who told me that her current main source of income was "seducing other men," said that she started hustling men while waitressing, saying that there were just so many "easy slays out there either working in or coming to restaurants" from whom she could obtain money using "fake stories" about the need for groceries or rent. Tess similarly scammed men or "went fishing," as she said, while tending bar, and obtained "all kinds of money for abortions, security deposits, and kids' clothes." Linda, who worked at the racetrack, which she said was a "bad idea for a recovering alcoholic," reminisced about crack parties with jockeys and customers.

Kristen started dancing at age 18, the same age she started sniffing heroin ("before [I] knew what it was,"), and stripped through her 20s and 30s until the "tips and big money stopped." Since that time, she had been engaged in prostitution, and she talked at length about the many "compassionate strangers" she had met, especially one bar owner and several of his customers, whom she serviced after hours for alcohol, drugs, and shelter. Finally, Donna and Shawna spoke of their introduction to hustling through men they met at "the joints" in Rochester, which offered a haven for gambling, boosting, and other forms of entertainment.

Show Me the Money: Jen, Shawn, Mary, Latasha, Sissy, Kimber, Sherry, Tracey, Shasta

I loved my childhood 'til I was older, then I saw it was poverty: I had what I needed but not what I wanted.

—Shasta

The nine women in this category all initially became involved in crime for the rather simple reason of greed: They first engaged in theft or selling drugs for the sole purpose of getting money or obtaining material possessions. Theirs was a lifestyle, initially at least, that was fast and included "money, cars, houses, brand name clothes, big screen TVs, and the club scene." The words *initially* and *first* are used intentionally here, because for the older women in this group, the fast and moneyed lifestyle they sought and lived was a thing of the past, as was their criminal skill, which I discuss in the next chapter.

Included in the group were eight African American women and one Hispanic woman, with an average age of 33. All were mothers, and five— more than in any other group in this study—still had custody of their children. Unlike the women in other categories, these individuals also were more likely to have gone further in school or graduated and to have early and extensive work histories, which for some provided the opportunity and setting for theft. Moreover, all but one had conventional and often high aspirations as children, which most others did not; both Jen and Shawn had as children wanted to be lawyers, Mary saw herself as a psychiatrist, Latasha wanted to be a pediatrician, Kimber a writer, Sherry a psychologist, Tracey a doctor, and Shasta a nurse.

The family backgrounds of these women also were far more stable and protective than those of other women in this study. The size of the nuclear family was generally smaller, with two or three siblings present, and relationships with extended members, who often lived in the same neighborhood and provided child care for mothers who worked, were more healthy and supportive. Although all but one of the families was challenged financially, with parents and guardians often working several jobs, and lived in areas rife with crime, they also provided good homes for the children, which included structure, an adult presence, religious involvement, and the provision of the best they could. Most described their family lives growing up as "good, perfect, normal, and loving." Latasha, for example, said that she was spoiled as a child, with a mom and grandmother who tried to give her everything they did not have. They were lenient, she said, and spanked her only once. Also, although these women reported incidents of adult domestic violence or rape in their lives, in contrast to women in other categories they had experienced little physical abuse and no sexual abuse as children.

Latasha grew up surrounded by family, as did Kimber, who also said hers was a religious family that spent 3 days a week in church. Tracey's mother was a functioning alcoholic who provided well for her and stuck by her during an early pregnancy at 16. Shasta's mother was a nurse's aide who, while doing cocaine on the side, never exposed her children to her drug use. Shasta did not learn of it until age 20, when someone called the house for money. Mary's mother also used crack, but while her husband was incarcerated she supported her children by working in laundries. At the time of this study, she was 12 years in recovery, Mary said, and cared for Mary's three small children.

Jen grew up with both parents present and employed; she often worked with her father, a self-employed contractor, managing his office. Sherry's mother worked two jobs while raising her two children in what was described as a "very ghetto area"; her grandmother provided child care for the children, including Sherry's baby, born when she was 17. Sissy also grew up in an area where all she "knew was drugs, pimps, hos, gamblers, and number writers." Born in Bedford Hills Correctional Facility in Westchester County, New York, Sissy was sent to live with her grandmother at age 4 weeks. It was this grandmother who cared for Sissy and her three siblings by selling dinners and working through her church. Sissy said that what "she did for one, she did for all, and she did her best," sending her to karate classes and singing lessons at a local music school. Shawn grew up in the suburbs of Baltimore with adoptive parents who were "bourgie [class-conscious] school teachers," she said. When she returned to her biological mother in Rochester as a teenager, she lived in the projects and experienced culture shock. At the same time, however, Shawn said she encountered the same "bourgie attitude" from her mother, who worked for the Housing Authority and had aspirations of leaving the city of Rochester.

The women in this category all expressed an early and intense interest in having the good life of money and things, and their initial hustles, both conventional and illegal, were directed at acquiring it. Latasha, for instance, who said she wanted to be a pediatrician as a child, gave up on this pursuit because of "all them years—I wanna see my money!" For the most part, petty and grand larcenies were what these women did, and they generally began their thefts in the home, stealing from a grandmother or mother. At the same time, however, the women in this category, who were all about making money and acquiring things, engaged in a variety of other hustles and unconventional means to achieve their goals.

As adolescents and young adults, these women hosted crack or after-hours parties in their apartments, charging people an admission and drink fee and paying neighbors not to complain. Many also dated dealers, much to the displeasure of parents, as Jen remembered, having been called "a top-class whore" by her father. Furthermore, they all sold drugs at a relatively young age and reported that their own initial use was generally limited to marijuana and alcohol, with some sporadic involvement in cocaine. Sherry, for instance, rented an apartment for a dealer and then worked a 12-hour shift selling drugs from that apartment. Shasta also let a dealer hold her apartment for a couple of weeks; later, she did the same thing herself, when she paid a crackhead $40 a day to use his house as a spot to sell drugs. Latasha, however, seemed to exceed all others with her cunning: She acquired a monopoly on sales to apartment residents in her building and told me "I've never seen anything in the Bible that says you can't tithe from drug money." These were women who expressed a strong sense of inde-pendence, self-reliance, and self-esteem. They said that they did not want to be dependent on anyone and could not "live off McDonald's wages and Section 8 [federally subsidized housing]," especially with their frequently expressed taste for nice things. As Sherry explained, "I had what I needed but not what I wanted. I was healthy, but unwealthy—that's why I sold drugs." They also seemed to have greater control over their own drug use; in fact the one woman in this study who was not involved with drugs was a member of this category. It was things and money, not addiction, that motivated these women to steal and sell drugs and even though they might have made more money more quickly by prostitution, and admitted as much, the women in this category reported no such activity early in their backgrounds. They could not sell their bodies, they told me, and there was no way that they wanted to feel like crackheads or appear "off the hook" (i.e., out of control of their lives because of drugs).

Challenged: Sherry, Debby, Chantell, Jean, Viv, Darla, Stephie, Yola, Pearl, Liz

[Growing] up was sad. I hated my life. I was the only one who grew up with mental problems.

—Sherry

To say that the lives of the 10 women in this group were difficult bor-ders on a gross understatement. They were marked by harsh familial vio-lence and by failure and frustration in school, the community, and the criminal world, with relief or a leveling of sorts provided only through early and extensive drug use. All of the women's offense histories included numerous mental health–related arrests, and the women did whatever

they had to do at the time—whether prostitution, larcenies, or jostling—
to obtain money for drugs. There were 5 African American women in this
group and 5 Caucasian women. One of the women was divorced, and the
rest were single, never married. Their average age was 36.7 years. All but
1 had children, none of whom lived with their mothers. Most of these
children had been removed from the women's care by child protective
service agencies.

The early lives of these women were particularly "chaotic and confusing," as Debby said. Three of the women were sent as children to family in
Rochester by their mothers in the South, and because of psychological and
emotional disabilities, four spent good portions of their childhoods in foster care or institutional settings, from which they frequently ran. Darla, a
51-year-old African American woman who walked around the housing
unit with sharpened pencils in an eyeglass case to protect herself, said her
mother sent her to Rochester from Florida in 1990 after her "brother and
them" started getting her high 5 years earlier. She moved from cousin to
cousin for a couple of years, and typically used to dispose of property they
had stolen, but she had mainly existed in a series of abandoned houses or
on the street.

Stephie always carries a box cutter to protect herself while on the street,
where she has been, on and off, for the past 10 years. She was born in
Arkansas, and it was there, at age 15, that she committed her first criminal
offense, using the box cutter on a man in bar who she said was physically
abusing her. Stephie subsequently was sent to a series of relatives in numerous states, until coming to western New York, where she lived with an aunt
whose husband repeatedly raped her, leading to an abortion at age 13.

Chantell, who was born in Rochester, was as a small child "put
around with family members" until she ended up living with a much older
brother, who sexually abused her. "Mom was partying, hanging out, and
my father was never in the picture," she said. Her mother would show up
"once a month or so" and deliver money or food. Sherry listed six placements between ages 7 and 14, saying she was "in at 7 and running at 8."
Jean likewise reported numerous out-of-home placements since age 8
and was able to provide both the dates she went into these and when she
"AWOL'ed" from them.

Most of the women witnessed or were the subject of much violence in the home, both as children and as adults. Stephie, who saw her mother killed at the age of 5, said that she "grew up with violence all [her] life." "If you had a problem," she said, "you solved it with violence. If you didn't fight back, you'd get a whippin' [at home]." In describing her childhood and family life, all Viv could say was that "[growing] up was really sad." Her mother was always running from an abusive, alcoholic father, she said. She then pointed to a large scar that stretched across her forehead and stated, "I've always had a complex about this—what happened to me?" She said her mother told her some years back that the scar was a result of a burn that was inflicted by Viv's father "during another drunken rage" when Viv was 4 years old and living in South Carolina.

Debby would either run away or hide when the "worst father you could ever have came home from work." "He was crazy," she said, "and once set the house on fire when he passed out with a cigar in his mouth." Pearl said her first arrest was for an assault on her mother, whom she attacked after the mother got drunk and threw things at her and her baby. She then took $500 from her mother and spent it on "booze and drugs." Liz, when asked about her childhood, which consisted of alcoholic parents who either fought constantly or were never home, said sarcastically that "it was so lovely, I didn't wanna go home." She "wouldn't go to school," Liz remembered, "because I was afraid [my dad] would kill my mother." She added that her grandmother finally "turned my father in," and she and her five siblings were placed in foster care.

For all but one of these women, the school experience could be described only as painful and humiliating. Only Debby, the one woman who liked her special education classes, saying they were "the only thing that kept me from going insane," graduated from high school. Three of the women made it to 8th grade, two made it to 9th grade, one made it to 10th grade, and one made it to 11th grade. Their expressed reasons for leaving school clearly captured what the experience had been like for them. Sherry said she hated feeling different in the "handicap classes," and Jean said she "just didn't know how to act."

Stephie, who always was in special education classes, repeated eighth grade three times and finally left with what she said was fourth-grade reading and math ability. Pearl never made it to high school, she said, "because [she] had trouble with kids picking on [her] calling [her] sissy and punk." Yola, who left school in the ninth grade, said she "just couldn't take it anymore, not getting along with people in school." Viv just "got tired," and Chantell's mother didn't "let [her] go to school." When asked if she liked school, Liz, who made it to the eighth grade, said, "I don't know. I was so disturbed. I was afraid of school."

Work experiences also were limited and, for most women, nonexistent. All of the women received some form of disability insurance, and when they did work they were paid primarily under the table, cleaning houses, cutting grass, and shoveling snow or clearing icicles from roofs. Darla said her apartment manager let her clean and put out the garbage. Viv generally worked for elderly women in the neighborhood, cleaning their houses and cutting grass. Liz said she was now working off the books with her new male friend, landscaping and delivering firewood. The only job that Pearl, who had aspirations of being a nurse's aide, could recall was being a bell ringer for the Salvation Army once, a long time ago.

With their histories of violence and personal frustrations and failures, what appeared to lead these women to their current street existence, which involved either prostitution or larcenies, were drugs and the feelings of "being normal" or "leveled" that these provided them. Also, for nearly all of the women, the introduction to drugs was made through people—men, associates, or family members—who cared for them. Stephie started cocaine at 15 because she "got involved with the wrong guy." Her oldest child's father told her "just try it—it'll help you not think of things." She continued to stay high "not to think about it" with people she knew, primarily "girlfriends who'd hook [her] up with guys to get high with." "I do it for drugs," she said. "It's the drugs that's pimping me." Chantell and Darla were both introduced to crack by the brothers who took care of them. Darla remembers asking her brother "What's that?", and "Before I could say no, I said whoa." Both now relied on friends, primarily other women who smoke, to get dates who will buy them drugs.

Viv was introduced to cocaine and then heroin by the father of her now-grown children. She continued to use "because of the way it made me feel. I'm a knucklehead. I'm afraid of things—but not when I use.

Then, I'm a big girl and wanna be out there." Viv's money for drugs came from prostitution "because I'm too scared to do anything else." Lisa also expressed much fear and she, too, engaged in prostitution for crack—"for the energy inside it gives me." She started smoking through a friend's brother—that's "when Satan jumped all over me," she said. Lisa said she continues to party and seek out partying on the street, in spite of the presence of a "good man, a mother hen in [her] life" now, because "there's a lot in my head. I get bored. I can't think straight."

Debby, who frequently rides her bike into the city to party or to have "one last joyride," as she said, traced her introduction to the street scene to an early pregnancy. "I left home," she recalled, "because my mom was angry. I met this guy [her fiancé, who was murdered in 1989] and he gave me some crack. It took the pain and anger away. And, I was happy, in charge—it was a thrill." Jean followed a somewhat similar path, but her stressor was having to provide child care at an early age. "I started smoking at 17. My son was 5 months old—I couldn't take it anymore. This guy gave me some crack. It leveled me—I need medical cocaine."

Just Another Addiction: Kay, Janie, Vicky, Althea, Cathy, Susan, Sabra, Edith, Norma, Bri

I was pregnant and a bad girl, just plain out rude. . . . If you wasn't tough or down, you'd get punked.

—Kay

When speaking of their initial reasons for why they committed crime, the women in this group almost sounded like they were explaining drug use. To a person, they provided detailed descriptions of their criminal activities that were punctuated by expressions of what they said were the euphoric feelings they experienced while committing crimes. Included in the group were eight African American women, one Caucasian woman, and one Hispanic woman, with an average age of 34.4 years. One was widowed; one was divorced; and the rest were single, never married. All but one had children, and only one of these mothers reported that she still lived with her children, the four of whom were now being cared for by her mother.

What appeared to distinguish this group from others was a relatively early rejection of childhood or the dependent status of being a child. These were women who said they "cut up" early because they felt grown or, as Kay remembered, "I was pregnant and a bad girl, just plain out rude." Norma recounted an early altercation in which she threw a bottle at two girls who she first said jumped her out of jealousy and then, rethinking the incident, said, "It was probably me, my mouth, standing up for myself." In explaining her second arrest at age 16 for motor vehicle theft, Edith said she had been "hanging out in a drug house with some guy, playing video games and we just went drivin' and ridin'." When she arrived home 2 minutes past a curfew imposed because of a previous offense, Edith punched the waiting probation officer and was charged with assault. Vicky, who said she "was always thinking of a good, honest hustle as a kid," remembered how she would steal from her father's wallet at age 10, "rearranging bills so he wouldn't notice." "I was very sneaky," she said, "and 4 years later, I took my dead sister's ID to [the Department of Motor Vehicles] so I could get a legitimate one."

Cathy "just couldn't stay put" with different "religious relatives in Rochester and Georgia" and remembered sleeping in neighbors' cars to "just get away from God and the Bible." Sabra likewise moved out of her mother's house at age 15 to live with a girlfriend and her baby, saying she and her mother were always fighting because of her older, married boyfriend. "That's when I started drinkin' and druggin'," she recalled and, explaining her second offense at age 17, an assault, said, "I wanted more money. I jumped on my son's father and cut him a couple times. It ain't like it is now—the state didn't pick it up."

For most of the women, this being bad or tough was a necessity in the neighborhoods where they grew up. "If you wasn't tough or down," Kay said, "you'd get punked [humiliated, disrespected, or mocked] or worse. You had to fight." Edith similarly remembered her neighborhood. "That's when it happened," she said. "A lot of drugs, guns, dealers, everyone on corners selling, boys—he's cute, he's making money. This is a blunt [cigar hollowed out and filled with marijuana], have some beer." Norma wondered "why everyone in [her] neighborhood was walking around selling food stamps and kids' clothes, 'til I tried [crack]." Janie said she "learned early that you got to live outside like you're inside—like I'm in jail. I protect myself, I have to be ready, that's why I got a gun." Althea described her childhood neighborhood with two words, *violence* and *drugs,* which were repeated by Bri, who also added the phrases "dangerous, rough, very ghetto. Peoples getting shot and beaten."

Cathy, who claimed she had been stabbed by her own relatives for money or drugs, gave an explanation for the violence and proliferation of drug houses in the neighborhood where she grew up. "It used to be mainly men," she said. "Now it's women with young kids and people 60 to 70 smoking—that's my biggest fear—dying while smoking. It just shows how bad the economy's gotten." Susan gave a different take on her childhood neighborhood on the northwest side of Rochester, which she and others now referred to as "ghost town" because of a recent enhanced police presence. "The men are dying or going to jail," she said. "They raised us in the game and all we know is the game. We're coming out. A woman has to be on it, to protect herself. We learn real quick and there's nothing worse than a deadly woman."

Family life was similarly unpredictable and dangerous, with words such as *drama, chaos, confusing,* and *nuts* used to describe it. Edith remembered a lot of strangers in the house, whom her mother, a drug user, allowed to come in and sell their drugs. She said she would often hide her mother's drugs and would take money from her so that "we could pay the rent." Edith recalled how her sister referred to their 35-year-old mom as "the oldest baby in the family" and that it was she, Edith, who was her "real mom." Norma became pregnant at age 13, at the same time her mother, who was "running the streets," was pregnant. It was Norma who took care of her mother's twins and her own child, after delivery. Janie described her childhood and family life simply as "not good at all," with a father who beat her heroin-using mother, an uncle who molested her as a child, and a mother who Janie said was "jealous of me and always said 'you ain't never gonna be nothin'.'"

For all these women, home environments alternated between being argumentative and party-like, and all said they came from drinking families, with parents who liked to buy people or show their affection with money. "At first things were good," Sabra recalled. "My mom was a secretary at [a local] hospital until I was 10. After she lost her job, she got depressed and started drinking—then all hell broke loose." Cathy's mother also drank and was fired from her nurse's aide job when Cathy was 12. It was shortly after that that her father was "ordered away from the home" subsequent to finding his wife in bed with another man. Bri described a family life that consisted of "parties, music, playing cards, and fighting all the time." "It was good, though," she said, "because my mom kept us dressed and always got us things." Vicky similarly claimed that her "dad loved us with money and always entertained at home." She was "lucky and had it going on," she said, when her parents bought a bar and she "could party there all night with friends."

School was not very important to the women in this group, and for most it was referred to as "just an interruption" that prevented them from "doing their own thing," as Sabra said. They often "went in the front door, and out the back" on a daily basis, as Sabra remembered. However, most did not leave school of their own volition or because of pregnancy; the majority were expelled or thrown out for fighting or attitudinal problems. Also, although all but one of the women reported some history of childhood victimization, more than half said that they were often the abusers of men and, in several cases, the protectors of women.

Kay, in particular, who described herself as a "verbally aggressive" child who manipulated her father over her mother, said she was an abuser of past boyfriends and "detested" women who played "the dumb role," and especially those who "allowed" men to beat them. She seemed to cast herself as a defender of women who sought to empower them as well. Kay claimed that she stabbed one male abuser "on the block" three times, telling him, "If you ever hurt her again, you're gone." She said she then turned to the woman and told her something similar: "If you ever let another man hurt you again, you're the one who's gone."

Janie also claimed to look out for women on the street, especially prostitutes, saying that her street name was "Little Pimp." On the streets for a year and a half, she said that she would sit in the park and watch over the girls, "copping drugs" for them and stepping in if something turned violent. Bri's stabbing of one male friend has already been described. She also listed four others by name whom she had "cut up" over jealousy or anger for selling her stuff for drugs. Althea likewise distrusted men and called herself an abuser of men, and she recalled how she had left her "husband after beating on him" when their son was 2 days old, after she received "charge card bills that weren't mine," which included charges for clothing items she obviously would not have used while pregnant.

When Cathy quickly explained why she had committed her first offense by saying it was due to her "being of the street," she provided a fairly accurate and meaningful description of who these women were and why hustling was such a high for them. "Posting up," as Althea called her aggressive stance and readiness to fight as a child, was learned on the street, as was her ability to manipulate people with words. Explaining how she got involved in selling drugs at 17, Kay said,

> I was cool. I saw everyone on corners selling, so me and my sisters started. If only women sold drugs and not men, there'd be a lot less crime, less murders. There's womens out there, but too many play the dumb role, sell for him, let him use their house.

These were self-described tough, sneaky women for whom survival was never guaranteed but always at issue and highly dependent on personal smarts and toughness. They loved drinking or drugging, which started, on average, at age 15, and reputation was important to them, as were the street characteristics of cunning and hustling that garnered it. That they might feel powerful and euphoric when succeeding at their own particular criminal hustle seems very understandable in the context of lives marked by unpredictability, with little protection or control, and neighborhoods where the mentality of survival of the fittest prevailed.

Lives of Loss and Trauma: Judy, Cindy, Cora, Lani, Tonya, Marsha, Dina, Jenna, Cody, Libby, Tasha

The street is reality turned inside out. We are all just trying to fill the void, first with money, then drugs, and finally, sex.

—Judy

The 11 women in this group appeared to be the most personally and emotionally damaged of all women in this study. They had experienced many losses and the most trauma in their lives, and they frequently referred to these incidents as "turning points" when explaining their involvement in crime and drugs. All grew up in households in which domestic violence was a constant, and all had experienced sexual abuse as children. As a group, the women were older, on average, than the women in the other categories, with a mean age of 37.7 years. There were 7 Caucasian women, 1 African American woman, 1 Native American woman, 1 Caucasian–Hispanic woman, and 1 African American–Hispanic woman. Three of the women were childless, 2 had grown children (one of whom had been murdered), and the remaining 6 had lost custody of their minor children after being charged with endangering the welfare of a child. Four were divorced; 1 was married; and 6 were single, never married.

The early family lives of these women were marked by extreme rejection and disruption. All reported mothers who were suicidal, depressed, involved with drugs, or angry, and fathers or stepfathers who were alcoholics or addicted to drugs as well as sexually or physically abusive. Three of the women reported being abducted from the family home as children by their fathers; one was taken from the reservation of her birth, and two were removed to the father's country of origin: one to Turkey and the other to Italy.

In describing their childhoods, the most common words and expressions used by the women were *lonely, depressed, scary, alone, motherless, withdrawn,* and *sad.* Cindy was echoed by all when she said her family life was "difficult and insecure, physically, emotionally, and spiritually. I didn't know what was coming next." All of the women were quick to point out that their siblings had fared no better than they as members of these families. If not deceased or incarcerated, most of the women's siblings were "alcoholics, drug dealers, or living with some crackhead." Furthermore, there seemed to be much guilt and deep-seated anger among these individuals, much more than in the women in the other categories, and both of these emotions were expressed frequently and often with great emotion during their interviews.

Within this group, only two women reported liking school. Judy and Marsha just got high and escaped from the school routine. Libby hated it because she felt different not having as much as the other children, as did Tonya, who, because she grew up in a trailer park, felt like an outcast among her suburban peers and used to get sick every day before going to school. As she got older, she marked herself as different, first with a mohawk and then as a goth, which she emphasized throughout the interview by repeatedly saying, "Screw the rich people." Cindy dropped out in 11th grade because she was not "comfortable around people and was drinking a lot." Cody stopped going because she was ridiculed for sucking her thumb and because she had a rash around her mouth caused by licking her lips so much.

The only aspirations that these women said they had as children were to "get out of that house as soon as [they] could and to stay high." All of the women met these goals. Several ran from home and school and were adjudicated and held as Persons in Need of Supervision in juvenile detention facilities, and they all were on the street by the time they were 17 years old. In addition to their far worse family situations, these women differed from women in other categories by their early and extensive drug and criminal histories.

All had started using alcohol before age 15, and all were polysubstance abusers, having dabbled in LSD, mescaline, cocaine, methadone, and heroin. They had been in rehabilitation many times, and several now lived with associates met through various clinics. In fact, they described rehabilitation with the same words they used to describe jail: that it was their revolving door.

The women's times in jail were far more numerous and regular than those of women in other groups, and their criminality was far more diverse and typically included several crimes of violence. Among the charges these women incurred were the following: larceny, drug possession, prostitution, panhandling, resisting arrest, disorderly conduct, possession of stolen property, criminal possession of a weapon, robbery, endangering the welfare of a child, and assault. The lives and words of three women—Judy, Tonya, and Tasha—exemplify this pathway into crime well.

Judy was a 47-year-old Caucasian woman from a working-class background who, when asked how many times she had been to jail, responded, "Oh my God. At least 25 times." She claimed that her mother, whom she called "Mommy Dearest," was "vain, beautiful, and very physically abusive." The woman was "an alcoholic and full-blown suicidal," Judy said, and often told her "I should've aborted you." She was repeatedly molested by her grandfather, who said she'd "be dead before 18," and she claimed that her father was in the mafia, naming local operatives who had visited her home. She also said her father was a fence (i.e., someone who sells stolen property), remembering "deliveries of stuff" to the home and "refrigerators stuffed with cartons of cigarettes in the garage."

Judy started "avoiding school" by the time she was 12, and when asked what she had wanted to be when she grew up, she got visibly angry and said, "I don't know—What the hell, I had to fight for my life." She left school and home at age 15 to move in with drug associates in the city. Judy said that she had used "'most every drug out there" and that her drug of choice for the past 13 years was heroin. She said that since she was 16 years old and committed her first larceny, her life had consisted of going "back and forth to jail" and that her offense history included other multiple larcenies, prostitution, robbery, assault, and weapons charges. There was much more "back there," she said, for which she had not been caught and it was at that point in the interview that Judy became very suspicious of "where all this information was going."

I stopped the discussion after Judy became so visibly upset, placing pen and paper on the table between us. We spoke for about 10 minutes, with me reminding her about the purpose of the study, my university affiliation, and the complete anonymity of her participation through the use of pseudonyms and lack of specific identifying information (birth dates, addresses, etc.). After this, Judy responded, "I know, I know" and then calmly asked me, "What else do you want to talk about?" The interview continued, without any other interruptions or signs of discomfort, for another hour.

Judy was an articulate and very reflective woman who obviously had struggled with her past in numerous detention and rehabilitation settings. It was, in fact, on the basis of her account of her past and present lives that I labeled this pathway "Lives of Loss and Trauma." She said that "We are all the products of abusive families and we are all damaged in some way." The street, in her words, was "reality turned inside out—we are all just trying to fill the void, first with money, then drugs, and finally sex." When out there, Judy said, "I was a living dead person. Drugs kept me going and made me feel normal. I found a family, a way to live, to survive." At the same time, however, she said everyone on the street or a part of her street survival were "pimps in all forms" or an "asshole, from the cops to the bodegas [corner stores]." No one was to be trusted, especially women, who were "a threat to [her] survival, . . . next hit, . . . or next hustle."

Judy characterized life as being "like a pinball machine, where you just kept bouncing off things, going every which way, 'til you're down the chute." That course and chute were very much reflective of what she had experienced and seen as a child and was now living as an adult. "I grew up on the front line, fighting for my life," she said; "all the craziness at home—the people, their hatefulness, beatings, stealing, drugs, booze, all night bars. I was going back and repeating the same things as my family."

Tonya, a 31-year-old Caucasian woman, also was a very articulate and reflective young woman who, after hearing about the purpose of the interview, said, "Women's voices need to be heard in this patriarchal society!" Everything to Tonya was about struggle or the powerful versus the powerless and, because of her background, she was very conflicted as to which side she was actually on. Growing up in a trailer park, she felt like an outsider in her suburban school; at the same time, however, she was quick to point out in the interview that her "family was white collar." Tonya had nine larcenies to her credit, which she explained by saying, "Screw the rich people." She hadn't engaged in prostitution, because she said it was "too demeaning to women." Yet, in explaining her use of heroin, Tonya said, "We're the clean people. At least we don't geek out [act or behave uncontrollably] and pick at carpets. Heroin is a much more upper class drug."

Tonya's background included physical abuse by both her biological father and her stepfather. At age 2, Tonya's biological father abducted her and her sister to Turkey, his country of origin, where Tonya remembers a grandmother "squirting lemons in my eyes, because she saw demons." She also shared how her abduction to the Middle East was ironic, given her fondness for heroin. When Tonya returned to the United States, she said she lived in a house where she was not wanted, that the stepfather didn't want her there and how her mother put him first. Tonya left the house at 17, after she got into the punk scene, and lived with several friends in the city, surviving, she said, by "dumpster diving." Heavily into drugs, she said it was "awesome, like being in a gang." "Fag-bashing" in a local park was a favorite activity.

Tasha, a 39-year-old African American–Hispanic woman, was the survivor of an alcoholic father who repeatedly raped her between the ages of 6 and 13. Her mother, a heroin addict, hadn't been in the picture since she was 4. Tasha described her childhood as "chaotic, very scary," and remembered a time when her father came to school and punched her in the eye for talking to a boy. She ran from the home frequently and was placed in at least four detention facilities and one foster home. Her drug of choice was crack, which she reported starting at 13 years old. Tasha's criminal history was extensive and included many different charges, ranging from larcenies, prostitution, assaults, forgery, possession, and robbery. She said, "everything I did in the streets—I wanted to hurt [my father] as much as he hurt me."

CONCLUDING REMARKS

The city of which these women were residents, both as children and as adults, can only be described as distressed, both socially and economically, and marked by all of the social ills associated with extreme, concentrated poverty, including criminal violence, drug infestation, and structural and institutional deterioration. The disrupted childhood homes of the women reflected these ills, with parents who were marginally employed, frequently absent, often incarcerated, and involved with drugs or alcohol. As an aggregate, the women exhibited the personal outcomes of disorganized, abusive upbringings, evincing limited educational achievements, marginal employment histories, and a host of physical and mental health problems. In the midst of these apparent commonalities, however, I identified six analytically distinct pathways into crime through the comparative case method. Each pathway was distinguished from the others in terms of structural and process factors relating to the women's family backgrounds and childhood and adolescent experiences. In chapter 6 the groups themselves become the focus of inquiry, and I examine each for the nature and extent of the women's criminality over time.

6

Criminal Patterns and Lifestyles

The concept of "catching a good lick" was introduced in chapter 1 as one of the most commonly heard expressions among the women interviewed for this study. Somewhat synonymous with the words *hustle* or *scam,* a lick was both an outlook on life as well as a set of behaviors developed and observed by the women to survive on the street through criminal enterprise. As an attitude or mindset, the expression referred to having the wits, ability, and opportunity to con someone out of something of value with very little effort. It was, as Terri said, "when you did something bad, but got something good out of it." Although this might be construed as being somewhat of an amoral stance toward life and other people, it also, in the context of these women's lives, could be seen as a mark of industry and success whereby one did what one had to do, did it well, and survived.

This opportunistic attitude was clearly expressed by the women as they described each hustle of their criminal careers. There was much agreement among the women about the behaviors, activities, and skill sets necessary to achieve a safe and satisfactory outcome for particular criminal events, from prostitution and property offenses to drug sales. In other words, the women described very evident norms that directed what they did and did not do in specific offending situations or to accomplish a successful hustle.

In this chapter, I discuss the nature and patterns of these hustles. The units of analysis for this examination were the six groups or categorizations identified and described in chapter 5. Using information provided through intensive interviews, I developed profiles of the criminality engaged in by each group, from initial offenses reported by the women to those that followed, in an effort to discern apparent patterns in their criminal careers as well as differences among the groups and possible reasons for such variations. I used these qualitative data to learn about the how and why of the women's criminal activities. To learn about what the women actually did, and when they did it, I accessed criminal history information through the jail records system, which provided information on each woman's age at and nature of first arrest, number of arrests, nature of charges, and number of jail commitments.

After closely examining these different data, I found that the six groups of women were distinguishable from each other not only in terms of their backgrounds or pathways into crime but also with respect to offense histories, patterns, and lifestyles. For instance, whereas the women in some groups (e.g., Challenged, Lives of Loss and Trauma) evinced an almost frenzied movement among different offenses, those in other groups (e.g., Show Me the Money, Just Another Addiction) were typically able to modify their hustle, primarily because of personal characteristics but also as a result of access to criminal network resources within the community, in ways that seemed to capitalize on particular skills. Discussions of each group's criminal patterns and lifestyles follow.

ALL IN THE FAMILY

The women in the All in the Family group committed their first offense at an age younger than the women in any other group. On average, they were 17.5 years old at the time of their first arrest. Although they had been criminally active for an average of 19 years, the range of this activity was between 2 and 31 years. With two exceptions, these women began their criminal careers with property offenses, primarily petty larcenies. The two exceptions were women who reported charges of disorderly conduct. As a group, these women also had compiled the second greatest number of arrests, with an average of 33.4, as well as jail sentences, with an average of 17.2 stays reported. These numbers are in all likelihood due to the average age at which the women started in crime, their average age at the time I interviewed them for this research, and the average time that they had been criminally active.

As I have stated, their beginnings in crime were primarily rooted in property offenses. Also, they seemed to learn to do from family: grandparents, parents, aunts, uncles, and cousins, hearing stories in their homes or actually witnessing or participating in criminal events. Pat, for example, said she started boosting when she was 7 or 8 years old and that she boosted with cousins in whatever neighborhood she was living at the time. The hustles these women learned from family members were not limited to illegal behaviors; they also included somewhat unconventional ways of making money rooted in the underground economies of their neighborhoods. These ranged from grandmothers selling dinners from their kitchens to basement card or drinking parties where a price of admission and fees for services were charged. What these women seemed to learn from family, in other words, was not only the mechanics of particular crimes but also an attitude or outlook on life and survival that condoned hustling or catching a good lick.

The initial lick for women in this group was boosting. Initially these women stole not to support a drug habit but because it was what they knew, what they were good at, and what they said they enjoyed. To a person, the women characterized their early days of boosting as being a job, one that required numerous personal and interpersonal skills but that also was fun and usually done, at least at first, with and for other friends and family members. They recalled their favorite stores for stealing; the time of day they started, usually early morning, when salespeople were busy opening or visiting with each other before the first mid-morning rush of shoppers; and how they did what they did, which always included an emphasis on personal appearance, prior knowledge of the store's layout, and a plan for entering, shopping, and leaving.

For most of these women, their early days of boosting were also very much a social thing. They "shopped" with female friends or cousins, with everyone having a particular role in the enterprise, be it as a cover, a friend with whom one was arguing to serve as a distraction, or a companion the woman was rushing to meet in the checkout line. The women usually targeted items to steal not on the basis of need, value, or to finance one's drug use but because the merchandise was for someone, either as a gift or as something that been preselected by the person. As the women grew somewhat older but were not yet drug dependent, they reported less direct involvement of others in their shopping sprees and were more likely to steal not for gifting purposes but on order, to pick up items for an established client base, which usually comprised friends or family. Many reported having a specialization in what they were good at stealing, such as Cathy, who called herself the "Perfume Lady," recalling how "easy it was to drop display bottles in a bag" and how easy these were to get rid of, because "everyone likes to smell nice."

The lifestyles of these women in their early years initially contributed to their success as boosters. These lifestyles were "fast" and typically involved the club scene in Rochester, where they wore, took orders for, or sold their wares and partied. These lifestyles, however, invariably led to a woman's demise as a booster as she became more involved with drugs and more reckless or unable to plan and execute thefts with the finesse and caution of her earlier days. As she aged and became more drug dependent, the "job was no longer exciting," as Pat recalled, but "became driven by my drug habit." Pat took more chances, going to stores that in the past had been avoided because of store layout or security level, was less aware of and attuned to the routines of store personnel and security, and was more likely to panic and not "finesse a quick exit," as she remembered.

The women also said they were not as selective in what they "grabbed" and often "got stuck with stuff they couldn't get rid of." Although the women reported that by this time they were more likely to work alone when stealing, they also said that they often had to depend on others for a pickup from the store. It was these others, usually "some crackhead paid with drugs for the use of their car," who often posed them additional problems, by not being where they were supposed to be when a speedy exit was necessary.

The results were more apprehensions and times spent in jail on larceny charges, as well as other offenses reflective of their state of mind at the time, and changed modus operandi, such as possession of stolen property, resisting arrest, disorderly conduct, simple assaults, and a variety of motor vehicle offenses. Increasingly involved with drugs, these women also accrued more possession charges and other offenses, such as endangering the welfare of a child, after which they typically lost custody of their children through the actions of child protective service agencies.

Most of the women changed their criminality somewhat or modified their lick or hustle at this point in time or as they aged and became more drug involved. Some of the women continued with property crimes but limited themselves to stealing and forging checks obtained from mailboxes or, as in the cases of Doris, Elisa, and Karla, from elderly clients for whom they cared in jobs that paid under the table. A few, such as Esther, Marie, and Kate, committed car thefts. However, many more became involved in panhandling and the various ancillary public order charges associated with it, such as menacing, harassment, and disorderly conduct. Only three moved on to prostitution, with one charge each, such as Marie, who said, "To boost, you need to look okay. When I'm using, I don't—I'm skinny, nodding out. It's just easier to hook."

PARTIERS BY TRADE

The Partiers by Trade women experienced their first arrests at a much older age than women in the other groups. On average, they were 25.7 years old when they were first arrested, and they had been criminally active, on average, for 13.7 years. With two exceptions, their first offense was prostitution. The two exceptions included women who were arrested for grand larceny and driving while intoxicated. The average age of the women at the time of their interviews for this research was 40.2 years. These women had the most arrests of any group, an average of 41.5, and the most jail commitments, an average of 22.4. Given that these women were older when they started in crime and the oldest, on average, of all study participants, the volume of their arrests and jail commitments seems to be explained by the very public nature of their offending behavior.

The early lick for these women was hustling money from men met at their jobs as coworkers or clientele, saying they needed the money for rent, food, or necessary medical procedures. Sexual favors sometimes, but not always, accompanied these hustles. Jess remembered a cook where she waitressed and how she "made fake promises" and spoke of her phony need for groceries to hustle him out of money. She called him and another older man who still dropped money off to her every time she was in jail "easy slays." Tess likewise had a man she met while waitressing pay for "two abortions and two security deposits." What you had to do, Missy said, was to "let them think they're taking care of you—that they're your hero."

For many of the women, the progression into pure prostitution began with their introduction to Rochester's after-hours gambling joints and several hotels and social clubs in the area that serviced men from all walks of life with sex, alcohol, and drugs. A number of these "hooker clubs" and "hooker havens," as Shawna called them, remain open and in business, known to—and, according to the women, sometimes frequented by—local law enforcement officers. Unfortunately for most of the women in this group, these clubs and hotels, where Saundra remembered servicing "gypsy workers" (i.e., itinerant laborers in town for various construction projects), were a distant memory of some 20 years ago. That is because their addictions had progressed to the point where the women were quite visibly damaged physically; these women, in their 30s and 40s, looked far worse than individuals much older, with lost teeth and frail, haggard appearances. All were now on the street or "walking the track," as they called it, where their lick was quite different and far more dangerous.

All but one of the women worked an area of Rochester known for prostitution activity, because, they said, that was where the money was. The exception, Elise, who called herself a "hippie child" at 35, had tried to work this area but couldn't "'cause all the women had knives." Being wild and partying was no longer the objective of the women at this point in their lives; their mission now was to get money and drugs "to stay off dope sick" or "to get off E" (i.e., to feel normal by getting "off empty" [i.e., off drugs] or obtaining drugs; see chap. 1). Their days typically began early—if, in fact, they had slept at all—and always started with their first hit or "blow," usually obtained on credit from a known dealer in the neighborhood they worked. Nobody kept any drugs on them for this purpose of a "wake-up call," because nobody could hold back from dipping into it before they actually needed to. Once they had done their first date, it was the dope dealer who was paid back first, and a second hit was obtained, along with a few loosies from the corner stores. The women then returned to their spot on the street; they usually worked particular blocks or locations to catch another lick, which they hoped would be a good one.

For these women, a good lick was not just a date—it was getting paid well by a man for doing as little as possible, whether it was just showing him some body part or talking him through a sexual act. Some of the women had regular customers; most did not. A good lick also was someone who provided the women with perks such as cigarettes, food, or scratch-off lottery tickets and bought a motel room for a couple of hours, thinking he would get more as a result. Car tricks, although less preferable, were far more frequent. Even less desirable was servicing drug dealers, which all of the women said they had had to do at times to fend off being dope sick.

A good lick also wanted to party with the woman and would furnish her with money to buy drugs. She did this quickly, having a relationship with a known dealer who, in exchange for the business, would provide her with an extra bag for herself, or so each woman claimed. This did not mean that she returned the full amount of her purchase to the date, however; all of the women said that, depending on their assessment of the man's familiarity with drugs, they would dip into bags or tell someone a dime bag was actually a twenty. Finally, a good lick was someone who could be easily and safely victimized. All of the women reported "vicing" (i.e., victimizing) dates who presented the women with the opportunity to do so. These were primarily out-of-town dates and dates the women met in motel rooms. It was a maxim among the women that one did not vic regulars, because that would result in a loss of business; also, one did not vic car dates, because they could subsequently drive around and find the woman, with results that could be far worse.

Details also were provided about bad licks, including types of transactions, men, cars, and locations that were avoided by most of the women. Although all said they had exchanged sex for drugs, all similarly expressed their displeasure at having to do so, saying it made them feel like a "crackhead" and that a person lost respect for doing so. Men who drove beat-up vehicles or walked to solicit them also were avoided, the former being seen as rough or cheap and the latter as dangerous or suspicious. Parking lots were preferred over parks because of the former's visibility, and although all of these women had, when desperate, engaged in sex in crack houses, these venues were among the least frequently used because of danger and loss of status and because the women did not want to be tempted to smoke up their profit.

As stated earlier, most of the women first began prostituting in the relatively protected venues of social clubs and after-hours bars or gambling joints. This might explain why their first arrests occurred at the older age of nearly 26. These arrests typically occurred on the streets of the area known in Rochester for prostitution. As the women became more involved with drugs and worked these streets instead of other venues, their lick changed, as described earlier, and included a diverse array of other illegal activities, especially those relating to vicing and partying with dates.

Because of these other activities, the women in this group had accrued a wide variety of charges in their criminal histories, including larcenies, possession of stolen property, unauthorized use of a motor vehicle, forgeries, and possession or sale of a controlled substance. As mentioned in the beginning of this section, these charges were in addition to the ancillary charges associated with their now very public and street-level criminal lifestyles and included disorderly conduct, loitering, panhandling, and trespassing. As the women aged and progressed in their drug use, compromising skills at identifying or outmaneuvering law enforcement officials and appearing in court with ever-increasing criminal histories, it was often these other charges, usually drug possession and larcenies, that typically brought them to jail. Tess and others bemoaned this fact, saying how "pros charges" (i.e., prostitution charges) were "a nothing—at most you caught 60 to 90 days. A petty larceny or [drug] possession charge was something else, altogether."

SHOW ME THE MONEY

The average age of women in the Show Me the Money group at the time of their interviews for this research was 33 years, the youngest of all study participants. The first arrests of all individuals in this group were for either property or drug offenses. On average, they were 20.8 years old at the time of this arrest, and they had been criminally active (again, on average) for 12 years, the shortest time of all groups, which perhaps is a reflection of their younger average age. Probably because of this, they also had the fewest number of arrests of all the groups, an average of 22.4, and the fewest number of jail commitments, which averaged 9.4. Although age may be one explanation for their limited official criminal involvement, another possible explanation was the level and nature of personal qualities and skills evinced by these women. Most of the women in this study had different types and degrees of cunning and resourcefulness; however, it was the individuals in this group in particular who appeared to have the most going for them in terms of wits, versatility, self-control, and actual business acumen.

The primary objective of women in this group was money, obtained quickly and easily, and the good life of possessions associated with it. As Latasha said of herself and her friends, "there are a lot of hers [a lot of women like her] out there. If you come to . . . our houses, you'll see it all, computers, flat screen TVs, vacuums, Old Navy, Timbs." The women initially did one of several things to achieve the fast lifestyle they all sought: They either stole from their jobs, shoplifted, or sold drugs. However, they did not limit themselves to specific licks, and unlike many of the other women in different groups, moved easily and frequently among criminal activities. All had some type of theft in their backgrounds and, more significantly, all reported selling drugs at some point in their career, even if they had not been apprehended for doing so.

Shasta, Latasha, and Tracey began their criminal careers by stealing from their places of employment or employers. They were profiled in chapter 5 for their similarities in background or "coming up" and the methods they used for accomplishing their lick, which was to obtain money quickly, with nothing between them and it. Shasta, who kept saying, "I likes money" during the interview and repeatedly reflected on how smart she was at using the men in her life for their money or positions, said flat out, "I don't do petty larcenies. I steals money." She began by forging checks and then stole and used the credit cards customers had left behind in places where she worked. Shasta also claimed to be "good and fast" at stealing cash from the numerous stores where she had been employed. Tracey likewise stole and used credit cards, beginning with her boss's credit card at a shoe store where she worked and progressing to bank cards, the last of which netted her nearly $8,000 and a year in jail for grand larceny. Latasha also used her job for stealing the credit cards of customers; however, she claimed that she worked in conjunction with three other women at various stores in the county, moving cards around among them and shopping at each other's establishments.

In contrast, Jen, Sherry, and Kimber all began their careers in low-level crime with petty larcenies, stealing merchandise from stores that they then boosted for money. At first it was money that was their sole motivation for theft. Jen, a 51-year-old African American woman who claimed to have been one of the best boosters in Rochester, a reputation that was confirmed by several other women in the jail, was particularly descriptive of this lick of her early days. She said that everything she did back then was preplanned and that she would go from store to store every day for at least 8 hours. Using a boosting girdle (i.e., an undergarment), Jen said that she could steal almost anything, even fur and leather coats, and that the trick was "all in the fold." She was careful with what she stole, however, because she "didn't want to get stuck with anything," and over time she built up a clientele for her wares. This clientele included "people with good jobs" who placed orders with her for merchandise as well as dealers; pawn shops; and, later in her career, corner variety stores, "[which] would buy just about anything."

Mary, Shawn, and Sissy displayed similar levels of motivation, as well as rationality, in their early offense histories of selling drugs. Sissy, for instance, said she preferred to avoid petty larcenies, because one always had to worry about getting rid of what was stolen, and sold drugs instead, because it was "quick, fast, easy money." She began selling from a rented room in a crackhead's house for which she paid $40 a day. She then obtained her own apartment, which she said was perfect for selling drugs. Sissy called it "the Hole, back in the cuts [on the backstreets or alleys]," with "lots of alleys or shortcuts to get into and out of it." Women were better at selling drugs, she claimed, because they had "more places to stash them" and were "smarter than men." Saying, "It's just like Adam and Eve," she added that the police were "less likely to mess with me. There I stand, pretty, in a dress and heels, telling the cop, 'I'm talking to him because it's my baby's father, Officer. I don't want no problem. I'll leave, Officer.'" Mary voiced similar observations, asking, "Who would you rather buy drugs from? A pretty woman or some kid on the corner?" She had corrected her first mistake of selling drugs out of her own home, from which she was evicted, and was now driving to outlying counties, where she charged twice what she had in the city.

In fact, all of the women in this group reported early involvement in drug sales and, with two exceptions, which I discuss shortly, all had either continued in this path or were now engaged in a variety of property offenses, including forgeries, pretty and grand larcenies, and welfare fraud. Mary and Shawn at first appeared to be the two exceptions to this finding. Both, like all others in the group, reported early and extensive involvement in drug sales. At the time I interviewed her, Mary was in jail on prostitution charges, and although Shawn had never been arrested for such, she said sex work was one of her current licks. However, on closer examination both Mary and Shawn's entry into and involvement in prostitution were decidedly different than those of other women in the study, especially those in the Partiers by Trade group.

For example, Mary seemed to be using the connections she had made while prostituting as a springboard to getting back involved in the selling of drugs. Saying, "My pimp's my pockets" and claiming that her street name was "The Money Maker," Mary said that she was now in business with the one dealer from whom she used to cop drugs for her dates who wanted to party. Like most others, she started by getting kickbacks for the purchases she made for these dates; however, she had progressed, Mary said, to working directly for the dealer, driving him to towns outside of Rochester for which she was paid "in weight" (i.e., in drugs), which she now was beginning to sell. Moreover, although Mary secured drugs for most of her dates, she, unlike other prostitutes in this study, said that working and smoking at the same time was something that she did not and would not do; she had control of her use, she claimed, and that a "lotta of the girls don't like me" because of that.

Shawn, who said that she had hustled drugs and boosted with her husband until he was incarcerated last year, claimed that she was now tricking "at the end of my run" but had never been arrested for it. Saying that her nickname was "Queenie," she added that she was now hooked up with another man, who sold crack from her house. A heroin addict, Shawn explained how this man trusted her with his drugs and money, saying, "I haven't screwed him yet," and how the two of them often "unbagged and rebagged" crack, to make the nighttime bags smaller than those sold during the daytime so they could turn a greater profit. Shawn said that she had designated two bedrooms in her house for women to turn tricks, as long as they bought their drugs "from us." Her own prostitution was limited to working with this man, who, like Mary's dealer, traveled to a town outside of Rochester where he sold drugs in a bar where he had connections. Shawn and another woman went with him, ostensibly to trick in this same bar, but she said she engaged in little prostitution and instead received a "finder's fee" for connecting drug-using dates with her dealer friend.

CHALLENGED

The average age of the Challenged women at the time of interviewing was 36.7 years. Their first arrests included petty larcenies, assaults, harassment, and prostitution charges, and their average age was 21.5 years. The average numbers of arrests and jail commitments that these women had experienced were 28.6 and 12.6, respectively, and they had been active criminally, on average, for 14.2 years.

What seemed to underlie the criminality of these women was a deep sense of desperation and an intense desire to "just escape." More so than other women in this study, the individuals in this group reported early and extensive drug use, with many saying they used drugs because doing so "leveled" them or made them "feel normal." It was these women, also, who were the most likely to report that they committed their crimes solely because they wanted to get high. Also, what they did in terms of crime very much depended on the circumstances they were in or the opportunities they had at the time, as well as their mental or emotional state. In other words, these individuals, much more than other women in the study, had a diverse career of criminality that from its very inception was shaped by both situation and state of mind and, instead of reflecting any rational modifications or progression, included numerous charges in no particular order of petty larceny, prostitution, disorderly conduct, harassment, drug possession, and simple assault.

The contours and venues of their illegal activities also differed from those of women in other categories. For instance, all said they often exchanged sex for drugs, which according to most other women in the study was the mark of an amateur or a person who was desperate and did not put business first, smoking up whatever profit was to be had. Furthermore, unlike women in the other groups, only a few said they copped drugs for their dates, depending instead on the man to obtain them. All also reported that they frequented and sometimes stayed in crack houses, where they dated as well as smoked, in contrast to most women in the study who said they did so only when they were truly "off the hook" (i.e., drug desperate, out of control).

The extreme urgency and risk taking with respect to the lengths to which these women went to secure drugs was reflected in the criminal charges they accrued, which most of the women explained by referencing the places and people of their truly desolate and drug-addled lives. Nearly all of the women, for example, had been "popped," or arrested while in drug houses, despite what were often poorly thought out efforts either to stay safe or to stay out of the system. All had drug possession charges as well as weapons charges. All also had charges of resisting arrest, menacing, and criminal impersonation.

The victimization of these women by friends, family, and associates also was pronounced and often resulted in them being charged with offenses that were not of their making. Whether it was holding stolen property or trying to dispose of it for others; being hooked up by friends; stealing items for family; acting as a lookout for drug houses in exchange for a little crack; being lured with the promise of drugs into cars, where they were victimized; or taking the blame for others who lied about facing state time if caught; these women were frequently used by the people with whom they associated, both friends and family. They also were the failures of the system, speaking disparagingly of all the "silly rules of drug court or probation" and how these were just "traps."

The criminality of Jean, Sherry, Darla, and Debby, all of whom reported near-monthly arrests for different offenses and a variety of mental health issues, including schizophrenia and bipolar disorder, panic disorder, and posttraumatic stress disorder, was particularly representative of the group.

Jean, who claimed that her nickname was "Kickboxer," said that her first arrest was for harassing the wife of the married man she was seeing. A crack user since age 16, she said the substance leveled her and hoped someday that there would be "medical cocaine." Jean also said, however, that the behaviors associated with using were almost as addicting as the crack. "Every single time I'm on a mission," she said, "it's an adventure." "Out there," she recalled, "it's all fun. We're not dummies."

Almost boasting, Jean mentioned how she particularly liked to "climb trees and smoke crack." She had even done it, she proudly (and with some degree of thumbing her nose) said, while sitting "under the billboard" of a particular business on the west side of Rochester, as well as on the "roof of a biker shop." Jean's other adventures, crimes, and licks included "stealing for friends in lower places," including her brother, a contractor in the city, for whom she stole merchandise from Home Depot that he allegedly sold to his friends. She would take whatever she could from stores, ranging from "boxes of candy, faucet sets, locks, and phones, always making sure [her] perimeter was safe," and then sell what she stole to the many people she knew "in the hood." When truly desperate for drugs, Jean said, she had no problem with exchanging "$50 worth of stuff for a dime bag" or engaging in prostitution in a "smoke house for a little crack," although she felt much safer on the street.

Debby's use of crack since age 22 also led to her frequent trips into the city, where she stood at bus stops to work as a prostitute, "since it didn't look as obvious," visited crack houses with dates, and "stayed up all night watching the house of a dealer friend to tell him when the cops were coming for a hit of crack." She had first heard about prostitution, she said, from an older sister "who always pointed out the women when we drove through that side of town." Debby had started hooking on "1 day a week— Tuesdays," when she rode her bike into town and stayed at the same corner, which she named, making sure not to walk too far, because that's "when the cops notice you," she said.

In explaining her forays into town, Debby said, "I do it for the thrill. To take all the pain and anger away." She partied with all her dates, Debby said, and "left it up to them to pick up the stuff [drugs]." Sometimes this backfired on her, like when she said she was beaten by "two guys who told me they'd pay me to get high and have sex with them." On what she said was her "one last joyride" into the city, which led to jail this time, Debby remembered riding around on her bike all night:

> I had sex with a Black guy for dope and just to get off the street. Then,
> I got a date for $40. This little kid on a bike came along and took me
> to a spot where I got more drugs. I went to a "user friend"—we par-
> tied a little bit, and he kept the rest.

The same desperate search for drugs and the adventure or escape they provided marked the lives of Sherry and Darla. Both drug-court dropouts (i.e., those who have failed the treatment-oriented drug-court program), they alternated their income-generating activities for cocaine between stealing and prostitution, with the latter being their primary lick. Both also reported extensive histories of harm on the street. Sherry, who said she had been on the street since she was 14 years old, about 20 years before, claimed that there were "very few pimps in Rochester." She named nine specifically, and said that, of these, six were still out there and three were locked up for assault or drugs. What had replaced them, Sherry said, were "wannabe pimps" or "simps,"[1] as she and others called them, "guys who watched the girls' backs, as they got their dates inside, smoked and robbed them—then took what the girls made, beat the crap out of them and smoked it up." Sherry's simp, the father of her last child, was in prison at the time of the interview for allegedly assaulting Sherry when she was nearly 8 months pregnant.

Darla, who had no simp and said, "I'm my own pimp," was a particularly sad woman. A 51-year-old African American woman who appeared far older than her years, she had been using cocaine since 1985 and did so, she said, "whenever I gets the money." Diagnosed with numerous psychological problems and having made previous suicide attempts, she had been alternating her living situation for the past 5 years between staying in a local park or abandoned houses on the northwest side of Rochester, when "I don't have no money or dope to go to some smoke house." It was in the

---

[1] An online urban dictionary (http://www.urbandictionary.com) defines *simp* as "a guy who acts all tough[,] like he doesn't care about his girlfriend around his friends but acts whipped in front of his girlfriend"; it contains the "root words of sissy and pimp."

latter that Darla turned most of her tricks; she also claimed that she often made a "little extra" there by watching people's kids while they smoked. As stated, Darla also reported an extensive history of harm on the street. She'd been beaten by "some young boys," she said, "who got her to get some dope." Her arm had been dislocated by a date as she leaped from his car after he bit her. She also claimed her own cousins had jumped her in an alley when she wouldn't give them her dope.

JUST ANOTHER ADDICTION

At the time of my interviews, the women in the Just Another Addiction group were 34.4 years old on average, the second youngest of all groups, and they had been criminally active for an average of 14.4 years. Their first arrests were primarily for petty larcenies; only two women had experienced another charge, and that was for drug possession. Their average age at first arrest was 19.3 years, again the second youngest of all the groups, and on average they had had 30 more arrests and 13.1 jail commitments. These women appeared to have more arrests than their average age and range of activity should have warranted, which may be explained by their expressed addiction to crime or the activity of one younger member, in particular, who was 19 years old and had been to jail five times in the past year.

In some respects, the offense patterns of women in this group were similar to those of two other categories: (a) the All in the Family group and (b) the Show Me the Money group. However, there also were distinct differences among the groups, the reasons for which appeared rooted in the motivations that underlay these individuals' criminality. Indeed, unlike other women in the study, crime for individuals in the Just Another Addiction group was not just about getting things, merchandise, or money. For them, what was as important as the criminal hustle was the opportunity that crime presented for the demonstration of personal competency, and this was achieved by seeking out criminal situations in which risk was common and served as a challenge for the women to display their abilities at catching a good lick through great cunning, verbal acuity, and much finesse.

Like the All in the Family group, the initial lick for these women was boosting. Although many of the norms and behaviors that directed their shopping were similar to those of the former group, others were quite different. For instance, for women in this category, stealing was not a social event, and it was done not to gift others with their wares: These women boosted, initially at least, solely because of the euphoria and self-esteem they experienced while doing it.

Most preferred to shop alone, not trusting others as lookouts or compatriots. Exceptions included women who worked with spouses, two of whom sat in wheelchairs the backs of which were used to conceal items, and individuals who paid someone, typically with drugs, to drive them to and from the stores. All indicated that they stayed away from "hood stores," where quality was low but security high, and preferred instead suburban malls and stores bordering the city.

Although most of the women in this group also spoke of going for name brands or quality items, saying that these were the easiest to unload, especially with the best customer named by all, drug dealers, they indicated that anything was fair game, from toothbrushes and razors to baby formula, depending on their need for money or drugs. The common and ready market for these sundries were the many corner stores that dot Rochester's inner city neighborhoods.

The early attraction of theft was well expressed by Janie, Cathy, Susan, Althea, and Sabra. Janie, who boosted for 7 years, described her typical day of shopping at the malls as being "beautiful," even though it always began "at the end of [her] run," with being sick and needing a first hit of drugs to get off E. Janie said that in her early days she would shop with a "list of what people I knew wanted" and that she hit only the "expensive stores with the name brands. I knew what shift to go on and when not to go. And, I could pop them alarms. Sometimes I even actually shopped, so I didn't look suspicious." A petite woman, Janie claimed she "wore big pants and a man's sweatshirt to hide stuff underneath. I'd put sneakers around my neck." Like many other women in this study, she claimed that some of her best clients at the end of her run were drug dealers. "When I copped drugs, they'd always ask 'You boost?'"

Cathy talked about the art of boosting and how it was all in the presentation, that one "could not walk in looking like a crackhead" and had to dress and act the part of a shopper with money. She'd have her nails and wigs, Cathy said, and would always pretend to be busy shopping, using her cell phone to have a phony conversation with someone about sizes, colors, or the number of items for which she was supposedly looking. "Boostin's what I do every day," Cathy said, and added, "If you're a good booster, people talk. They seek you out. I was good at what I did."

Sabra said stealing was easy and fun, at least in some stores, and she knew which stores to avoid. "If I have money, I [still] will steal," she said. "It's like an addiction." The same was true of Susan, who said she was a kleptomaniac and got a high out of boosting and would do so even with money in her pocket. Although she excitedly talked about how and where she stole, Susan's hustle or lick was not just about the act of stealing; it also included the art and thrill of convincing people to buy what she had taken. Althea also relished both the theft and its necessary aftermath of selling, saying she "felt like Santa Claus" after her last larceny, when she drove through her apartment complex and sold eight stolen bookshelf stereo units at half-price.

In contrast, Kay enjoyed the lifestyle of "sitting on the block and selling drugs," which "was better," she said, "than going to the clubs." She named five different locations and the years she had been at each and said that her last spot, of the activity for which she was now in jail, had been an abandoned house where she and five women, all pregnant like her, "sat on chairs, smoked blunts," and took calls on their cell phones for drug purchases. It was "beautiful," she said, "like a family thing" that usually included her young children sitting with her. "Who's going to bother a mother?" she asked. Kay sold small amounts and left it to her male partner to sell weight or large amounts, saying, "I like to sit on the block. Besides, I could be gone and I have four kids. Let the man do the driving and the big stuff."

What became of these women who expressed such an extreme attraction to crime depended on how deeply enmeshed they became in the lifestyle associated with it, that of drugs and fast living. In this regard, the patterns of their criminality resembled on some levels the findings cited previously for the All in the Family and Show Me the Money groups.

Like the All in the Family group, all but four of the women in the Just Another Addiction group had become increasingly involved with drugs and had progressed from larcenies to other property crimes that required far less presence of mind and skill, such as forgeries, welfare fraud, and car theft. At the same time, however, they periodically were lured back to the risk of their initial lick of boosting, with which they were now increasingly unsuccessful because of the toll that addiction had exacted on their abilities. These women ultimately ended up in prostitution-related activity to support their growing dependence on drugs.

In contrast, the four women who did not follow this path were like the women of the Show Me the Money group: They sold drugs, in addition to committing larcenies, and because of both their income from doing so and the personal skills they possessed and managed to retain did not become involved in prostitution.

Kay and Edith, for example, began their careers by selling drugs. Both reported limited personal use; Kay used marijuana only, and Edith, whose mother was a crack addict, said she would never use crack and only drank alcohol. Both also had been selling drugs since they were 16 years old. Kay, who was profiled earlier in this chapter, came across as a very strong woman: She "hated women who played the dumb role, selling for him or letting some man use their babies' house." She was also very cautious about and skillful at what she did. She stuck to very small sales, unless she knew the person, and did not like to show what she had (i.e., she didn't want to "look big time"), in terms of either money or quantity, on the block where she sold. Kay also knew how to "cook and cut" and said she preferred to buy her drugs in Florida or Georgia, where the prices were cheaper; to do so, she and her husband and kids traveled there, looking "like any other family on a vacation."

Edith was much younger and new to the game, but she claimed she was learning fast from the boys she knew and her cousins. What she was learning, however, was questionable and seemed to portend a lengthy future for her continued return to jail. Unlike Kay, Edith was far less cautious and appeared to be totally caught up in the fast, risky lifestyle of the drug scene in Rochester. She enjoyed hanging out with boyfriends and cousins in the city's drug houses—watching the action and playing video game—where she had been busted three times in the past 3 months. Edith, who was only 19, also had been arrested twice for stealing cars with guys she had met and was "hanging with" at drug houses.

Two other women, Susan and Janie, had started their careers as larcenists but claimed they were now selling drugs. However, unlike Kay and Edith, both were current daily users of crack or heroin, and both reported that they sold drugs only with their male partners. Susan and her husband ran a drug house in another county, where the money was better, and Janie claimed that she and her boyfriend, who went by the name "Geechie Pimp," sold drugs only to prostitutes working in the northwest section of Rochester. When questioned about the street name of her boyfriend, Janie said, "There aren't no real pimps anymore. A pimp don't get high, don't beat girls, don't believe nothing a ho says. A pimp's supposed to bail girls out. No more. Crack is the pimp and the ho's the stem."

LIVES OF LOSS AND TRAUMA

Women in the Lives of Loss and Trauma group were, on average, 37.7 years old at the time of their interview, the second oldest of all groups in the study. Much more so than volume of activity (i.e., number of arrests and jail commitments), what appeared to distinguish the members of this group from women in the other groups was the variety of what they had done in their criminal pasts. This began with their first arrests: Three had been arrested for petty larceny, three for simple assaults, three for drug possession, and two for prostitution. Their average age at the time of this arrest was the second oldest of all groups, 23.8 years, and they had averaged 26.4 arrests and 15 jail commitments over an average 14.8-year span of criminal activity.

Three things further distinguished this group from others in terms of offense patterns and histories. The first was an almost frenzied movement between a diverse array of criminal offenses, which was apparent in both these women's beginnings in crime and the subsequent careers they pursued. The second distinguishing characteristic was that these women were far more likely than the others in this study to have committed crimes of violence or offenses against persons in their histories. The third and perhaps most interesting difference was their involvement with other people in committing crime, a finding that has typically been associated more with men than women offenders.

The diversity of these women's criminal careers seemed to reflect the pinball machine metaphor one of them, Judy, used to describe life in general. All had used a variety of drugs, saying they did so to numb the pain or guilt of their lives. Also, all had bounced from one crime to another, especially as they became increasingly involved in drugs. Judy herself had begun her 31-year involvement in crime with a petty larceny charge at age 16 and reported a variety of subsequent offenses, including prostitution, drug possession, criminal possession of a weapon, and robbery. She reported using heroin for the past 13 years, which had replaced her use of cocaine, which began in 1985. "My drugs were my God," she said. "I used [them] to fill the void, the emptiness in me."

Tasha similarly reported a 19-year career of "drinkin' and druggin'," which began with larcenies and grew to include multiple arrests for assaults, robbery, weapons possession, prostitution, forgery, and possession of stolen property. Cindy, who said she had used cocaine for 21 years, kept using the expression "revolving door" to refer to her times in jail and the daily trips she made to the drug house. She had 25 arrests for prostitution, several of which she claimed to have occurred within hours after leaving jail, and at the time of the interview, she was incarcerated for an assault on a neighbor. Cindy also had multiple arrests for drug possession and larceny.

Marsha, Lani, and Dina, like the other women in this group, also had lengthy histories of arrests for many different crimes. Marsha's history included larcenies, burglaries, harassments, drug possessions, and intimidating a witness. For Lani and Dina, arrests ranged from criminal mischief and prostitution to burglaries, larcenies, assaults, and criminal possession of a weapon.

As indicated in the preceding discussion, the 11 women in this group were far more likely than others in the study to have criminal charges of personal violence in their histories, a reflection and outcome, perhaps, of the greater harm and loss they had experienced as children. All, in fact, had been charged with actual or threatened violence in the past, including assaults, robbery, resisting arrest, criminal possession of a weapon, aggravated harassment, endangering the welfare of a child, menacing, and intimidating a witness.

The group was also distinguished from others in an even more telling and interesting way, however, and this was in the way they dated their crimes with reference to important people in their lives and in the way they, unlike other women in this study, were more likely to have committed their offenses with these significant others met on the street or in jail.

A woman "met in rehab" (i.e., a rehabilitation facility) was a roommate and associate in Judy's most recent arrest for burglary. Judy also recalled how in 2000 she taught another acquaintance from jail to boost and then subsequently worked with the woman until she died in 2003. In the month before she came to jail, Judy lost another significant other and criminal cohort in crime, when her "husband," a man met during one her many drug treatment stays, died of AIDS. He had been her "buddy, my family" throughout Judy's recent stretch of crime, which at first included prostitution, something she stopped after 8 months, when she was almost killed, and then panhandling, an activity she was good at, she said, because "I looked so pitiful." Judy's final description of her life on the street seemed particularly meaningful: "It was there that I found a family, a way to live, to survive."

Libby, a 30-year-old daily crack addict who described her residence as "on the streets," also had a criminal life marked by an almost frenzied movement between petty offenses and relationships formed in that venue. A mother of three and pregnant at the time of her interview, she said she "lived to use and used to live," and she described walking into a hospital emergency room to deliver her last baby after making sure she had a crack stem in her pocket for use after the birth. As Libby described her criminal history, which included numerous prostitution, larceny, drug possession, and criminal mischief charges, she dated each, like Judy, with the name of the man or friends who were present in her life at the time. She'd get "dependent on one, 'til he beat the shit out of me," and then move on to another, typically a date she had met while prostituting. Over her 7 years on the street, she said her "mom never said come home." Children were left with family and partners along the way, because she'd always be partying with someone else and never went back to get "the kids or my stuff."

In recounting their criminal histories, Tasha and Marsha, like Judy and Libby, also seemed to date each offense in terms of the people in their lives. They, too, were more likely to have committed crimes with others.

Tasha began prostitution with a neighbor early in her life. She then stole from convenient stores and barbershops with friends, usually female, all of whom she named. At one point, Tasha claimed she sold drugs, very early in her use, as she said, when she wasn't tempted to "dip into the bags." She was now mainly engaged in prostitution, with a "friend" who looked out for her, and claimed that she "had to go around the world to get drugs" because the dealers "care about me. They all say don't sell to Tasha. She can't control it. You're killing yourself."

For every crime in Marsha's history, including the most recent burglary of a grandmother's house, there was usually a male friend and a couple of female friends involved, all named and dated in terms of the length of time Marsha had known them. Although she mainly stole property or credit cards, Marsha also tried prostitution "for a minute" (a frequently heard and very meaningful expression among the women, which I explain further shortly), not to turn tricks but to rob men, which she claimed to have done with friends backing her up. She said, "[I am] 26 but feel like I've lived the life of a 50-year-old." Marsha also said that it was always her "friends" who turned her in to Crimestoppers or stole her stuff when she came to jail.

Cora stole; engaged in prostitution; and panhandled while high, which helped with her depression and made her feel that she "could handle anything." She typically did so with a "significant other," who initially helped her on the streets with dope and a place to stay, which was sometimes a room in another crackhead's house but more often a hospital waiting room, parking garage, or "under [a] bridge."

Cody, who said she had experienced "seven losses since 2003: two kids, my dad, grandma, auntie, and two cousins," claimed that "I can be off the Richter scale sometimes." This was evident in her criminal history, which included several assaults, all of which were directed at men with whom she was involved. Now primarily active in larcenies and prostitution, Cody said it was her mother-in-law who looked after her on the street, letting her shower in her house and giving her food. Like Tasha, Cody claimed that "one dealer stopped selling to me, saying I was too good. I sat with him and his girlfriend one time and watched TV and ate."

Tonya, who described herself as having been a 15-year-old heroin addict, said that her punk scene during 1988 through 1994 was "awesome, like being in a gang." Tonya ran to the street at age 17, where she lived with "some girl, my sister, and a guy." She started "boosting with my man," who was now in prison, and has been on the street for 14 years. For most of that time, Tonya has lived and worked with other addicts whom she met through methadone clinics. Describing her typical day while criminally active, Tonya said,

> We wake up—usually four of us—everyone's sick, sniffling, if we don't have a wake-up. We open the phone book—when were we last here? We go there. Everyone fights about who goes in. We don't trust each other. We steal and get rid of it. We have money—then we argue over who's got the best dope. We get bags, park, and do it in the car.

While painting a less than familial or friendly picture of her associates, Tonya remained true to the description I provided of her in chapter 5: that everything was about class struggle or the powerful versus the powerless. "There's lot of exploitation of drug dealers," she said. "This one guy [who owns a game shop] tells us where to steal and what to get. He bailed my man out once to steal again."

CONCLUDING REMARKS

In this chapter, I have examined the six groups of women in terms of subsequent offense histories, patterns, and lifestyles. Each group was distinct from the others with respect to these factors. The bases for these differences appeared to be rooted in the early backgrounds and life experiences of the women, especially in terms of how they affected the women's progression into or protection from a later adult life of hard drug use and addiction.

I should stress that the majority of the women in this study did not begin their criminal careers because of, or to finance, drugs and addiction, as demonstrated by their initial offense histories and the often-intricate ways they committed crime. In fact, for many women it was the lifestyle associated with crime and the growing connections with people involved in it that led to increased drug use and addiction. Furthermore, sex work did not appear to be the ultimate outcome for all chronic, low-level female offenders, as has been assumed by some previous researchers. Also, by focusing on the context in which these women criminally operated, this study indicates that interpersonal connections, and not just those with men, have a role in the female offender's criminal career.

The preceding points are discussed further in chapter 8. For now, I move on to examine in chapter 7 the arrangements made by the women, as an aggregate, to survive on the street as well as in the jail. As I will show, personal resources and skill sets certainly influenced the life these women managed to eke out on the street. At the same time, however, there were numerous institutions, shared understandings, and street networks that not only played a role in providing the women's criminal opportunities but also greatly affected their survival and well-being while so involved. A discussion of these follows.

7

Surviving on the Outside
and the Inside

Approximately 15 years ago, the union representing the 500-plus jail guards in Monroe County marketed a t-shirt as part of their annual fund-raising efforts. Available in black or gray only, the shirt was embossed with the image of a typical cell, which was identified as "County Jail Bed-n-Breakfast." The t-shirts sold quite well—a reflection, perhaps, of the public's agreement with what seemed to be the apparent claim of the logo: that jail is too soft and inmates get treated far too well during their stay there.

At the time, I saw many other possible meanings behind the "Bed-n-Breakfast" logo, which I will not recall here. One of the more ironic to me was its not-so-subtle message about what jail had come to mean in the lives of petty offenders, that it was but a brief respite and increasingly normal reprieve from a life course of persistent low-level criminal activity and a marginal existence on the street. In fact, one could argue that in most urban communities the jail has become the equivalent of an emergency room for the criminal justice system, in terms of both the uses to which it is put by law enforcement officers and the triage and acute care services it must provide the clients it receives. This is especially true for the female clients, who because of lives marked by social and economic marginalization are generally shown to present more and greater physical and mental health issues on confinement. Jail administrators, in particular, have become painfully aware of these problems and the financial drain they pose to their meager budgets.

For instance, in 2006, the Bureau of Justice Statistics (BJS) reported that according to a 2002 survey of inmates in local (i.e., county) jails, medical problems were highest among female inmates, with more than half (53%) reporting an existing medical problem compared with about one third of the male inmates (BJS, 2006a, p. 2). Nearly one quarter of these women indicated they had more than two medical issues. In fact, women had higher rates than men for all medical problems listed except one, paralysis, for which men and women showed equal incidence. Among the highest problems female inmates reported were asthma, arthritis, kidney problems, heart problems, and hypertension. Female inmates also reported a rate of cancer that was 8 times higher than that indicated by male inmates (BJS, 2006a, p. 2).

Moreover, compared with the general population and other low-income women, jailed women have higher rates of recent and chronic substance use problems, HIV/AIDS, hepatitis C, sexually transmitted diseases (STDs), and mental health problems (Freudenberg, 2002, p. 2). A number of researchers also have documented the greater incidence of sexually related maladies, including a host of STDs, ranging from syphilis and gonorrhea to chlamydia, and chronic conditions relating to lifestyle, ranging from hypertension and diabetes to HIV and hepatitis among jailed women, as opposed to both jailed men and women in the general population (Centers for Disease Control and Prevention, 1999; Gellert, Maxwell, Higgins, Pendergast, & Wilker, 1993; Haywood, Kravits, Goldman, & Freeman, 2000; Holmes et al., 1993; McClelland, Teplen, Abram, & Jacobs, 2002).

Researchers also have found a higher incidence of mental illness among jailed individuals as compared with the general population in the United States. Teplin (1990), for example, found in her study of Cook County (Illinois) jailed men that 9.5% had experienced a severe mental disorder (i.e., major depression, mania, or schizophrenia) at some point in their lives, compared with 4.4% of the general male population. Even more dramatic are Robins and Regier's (1991, cited in Ditton, 1999, p. 2) statement that 6.7% of prisoners had been diagnosed with schizophrenia at some point in their lives, compared with 1.4% of the U.S. household population.

Data further indicate that the prevalence of mental illness among incarcerated people varies by sex. In her comprehensive report dealing with mental illness throughout the correctional system, Ditton (1999) found that within all types of confinement facilities, and among individuals on community supervision as well, women outnumber men in being identified as mentally ill. She noted that within jails in particular, 15.6% of men are identified as mentally ill, compared with 22.7% of women (p. 3). Other data show that women in jail are more than twice as likely than men to be identified as having some form of mental illness, the most frequent diagnosis of which is clinical depression (Pollock, 2002, p. 203). Even more disturbing are the higher rates of substance abuse and histories or prior physical and sexual abuse among inmates with mental illness (see Ditton, 1999, pp. 6–7).

More recent data provided by the BJS (2006b) on the mental health problems of inmates are far more troubling. The BJS reported that whereas 75% of jailed women had mental health problems in 2002, only 17% of all local inmates received any kind of treatment that year, with the most common form consisting of "taking a prescribed medication" (pp. 4, 9). Furthermore, BJS data confirmed other research indicating the high rate of drug and alcohol dependency among inmates with mental health issues, with 76% of all jailed inmates with mental health problems reporting such dependencies (p. 6). These inmates also were more likely to be repeat violent offenders, to have served three or more prior sentences, and to have been penalized with charges of violations for their inability to adapt to jail rules (pp. 8, 10).

I saw all of the problems discussed here and more among the individuals of this study, and it was, perhaps, because of these problems and the women's tendency to vocalize their need for treatment that they were seen as more difficult to supervise than men (see my discussion of this in the preface). Moreover, as I mentioned earlier, only 3 women reported that they had no medical problems to speak of at the time of the interview, and even they offhandedly indicated that they were depressed. This, along with bipolar disorder, anxiety, and posttraumatic stress disorder, were in fact considered "normal" among the women, with 55 of them reporting taking medication for one or a combination of these conditions. Almost as common was asthma. At least 7 indicated a diagnosis of HIV/AIDS, and another 5 said they had hepatitis C.

Among other physical problems the women reported were cancer (with one woman currently undergoing treatment for her third case), heart disease, diabetes, brain injuries, hypertension, lupus, aneurisms, glaucoma, kidney problems, arthritis, and a variety of STDs. All but one of the women also reported an extensive personal history of alcohol and/or drug use, and 90% of them ($n = 54$) said they had been using drugs regularly (i.e., on a daily basis) before this most recent incarceration.

Over the course of my time in the facility, I saw many women arrive in the unit. When they arrived, they usually looked awful—thin, ragged, toothless, and with numerous sores on their faces or bodies. Jail was indeed a sanctuary for these women (Fleisher, 1995). It was a place where they could get clean or just rest for awhile, have three meals a day and access to a shower, toilet, sink, and bed. Most received medications for their medical and mental health needs, but few saw a doctor, clinician, or therapist more than once, if at all. Some also might see a dentist (if they were there long enough and made their way to the top of the list), and a few actually could receive eyeglasses. At the same time, however, jail differed little from the street, with its meager provisions and the social interactions or behaviors of the women confined there. I discuss this, and much more about the women's survival strategies and mechanisms while on the street and in jail, later in this chapter.

THE ELEMENTS OF STREET SURVIVAL

Women in all six of the groups identified in this study came to share a common lifestyle of survival on the street, regardless of their pathway to it or their criminal activity while on it. In fact, what seemed to determine whether they had this lifestyle was not their familial resources or crimes of choice; it was instead where each woman was in terms of her own personal addiction that appeared to explain both her presence on the street and her embrace of a lifestyle or existence common to it to survive. Indeed, most of the women had become so involved with drugs that whatever bridges they had to their prior conventional and criminal lives (i.e., family resources in the former and criminal skill in the latter) were long since gone. When asked for their last residence, only 8 women told me they were not on the streets, and what these 8 seemed to share was a controlled level of soft drug use, limited to alcohol and marijuana, or no use at all, which only 1 woman in the study reported. For the 52 others, lives of crack or heroin use, interrupted by frequent stays in jail or treatment facilities, had destroyed whatever family ties they had and criminal skill they once claimed.

This is not to imply that the women's survival on the street did not require personal and interpersonal resources and especially street smarts, which very much described nearly all the women, even those who had some form of mental or psychological challenge. Most were self-described hustlers who, although their patterns of criminality differed, shared a common outlook, as well as a self-identity, of "being of the street." What this seemed to mean to the women was that they had the smarts, wits, and flexibility to survive and especially to stay "off E." They knew their way around and were well versed in the people, places, and things of the street as well as the numerous norms and institutionalized hustles that shaped not only survival but also encounters there.

Some women spoke of gut instincts or "having the devil in the belly" in terms of how they read potentially dangerous people or situations. Many more referenced divine intervention or just plain luck to explain why they were still alive. "It was God who brought me here, who made me stop," most said. At the same time, however, the women, to a person, almost seemed to pride themselves on their own abilities and wits as hustlers and survivors. In fact, something I stated briefly earlier and that was highly reflective of their versatility as hustlers was one of the most frequently heard expressions during this research: "and then I tried that for a minute." With their primary goal to secure drugs and stay off E, they all seemed to have an orientation to life and others in it that was very much rooted in their continued pursuit of catching a good lick, whether they were on the street or in jail. This hustling outlook of being able to spot an opportunity and outwit another of what one needed or wanted was the women's common means of survival in both venues.

The most important elements of street survival were staying safe; obtaining shelter or a bed, when possible and absolutely necessary; and avoiding dope sickness or staying off E. To protect themselves, most women carried weapons, usually knives or box cutters, and many described how they broke and used their crack stem for this purpose when confronted with a threat or violence. Most also had areas where they would not go or they avoided because of concerns for safety or the need for a speedy exit. Crack houses were one such site, for all but the Challenged group and women who were desperate for their dope. Stories about the drug-induced violence in these houses were plentiful, as were concerns about the traffic of strangers in and out of the houses and the possibility of arrest. Parks were avoided, except when used by the truly desperate to bed down, as were alleys, where visibility was lacking and egress difficult.

There also were norms among the women about people and situations to be avoided because of the danger they posed. Among the prostitutes, for instance, there were certain proscriptions about dating African American men, who were said to be cheap and often violent, and young men, who also were feared because of their potential for danger. "Drunks" were avoided (and most of the women did not like dating on weekends for this reason), as were men who were walking or driving beat-up, broken-down cars. Although these norms existed and almost every woman who engaged in prostitution voiced them and talked about their own gut ability to spot dangerous people and situations, all of the women recounted violence encountered on the street, and all said there was no possibility of staying absolutely safe while on it.

Drug-buying locations also were selected or maintained with safety in mind. Although availability was certainly not an issue, most of the women said they purchased their drugs only from people they knew, to avoid getting "ganked" (i.e., taken with adulterated substances or bags that were packed light). The majority also indicated that they preferred buying from known houses rather than on the street, where visibility was an issue and young kids predominated. They also spoke of what might be termed the "etiquette" of buying drugs from a smoke or crack house. One had to be known as a user, and one also had to use the right words or code names for making purchases, which were somewhat house specific.

Nighttime drug buying was avoided by some women, who said the bags were always "too light," and if drugs were credited first thing in the morning, one always paid the dealer quickly after her initial lick or trick. Most of the women also said there was a certain lifetime to drug spots in the city, and they talked with great detail of how long it took the police to target, investigate, and close down houses. The women liked to say they knew the "hot spots" in town, which they named and claimed to avoid. They also said they knew who, or what racial–ethnic group, controlled which drug or area of town, and they seemed to shop with this in mind, although racial preference was less an issue than quality.

Location also was an issue for safe drug using. Also, although nearly all of the women said they had frequented crack or smoke houses to use their drugs, most preferred not to use drugs in these settings because of the traffic of people, frequency of violence, and possibility of police apprehension common to the houses. Many also expressed concerns about the connotations associated with frequenting crack houses, that they were not and did not want to be perceived as being "crack fiends." The preferred setting for drug use was another user's house, an associate met from the street or a treatment facility, where one paid for a "spot" (to use) and possibly a bed for the night with drugs or $10.

When asked about sleeping arrangements, the most common response among the women was "Well, that's if I sleep at all." In fact, most of these women slept very little or only after several consecutive days of partying, when they would sleep for a day or days at a stretch. All had used shelters for this purpose, but very few liked them, equating the accommodations and people to "what you find in jail." A common alternative was staying with drug-using associates when they had the necessary "door fee" of money or drugs. As Elise said, "As long as you have dope, you can go anywhere. No dope, no door, keep walking." Although dope could get you in the door, one always had to be prepared for when the dope was gone. If the associate was a woman, "you'd better be out before the mailman got there; if a man, you can always buy some time with sex and then go."

When arriving on the street, some women slept in cars or vans, until those were stolen or sold for drugs. Many slept in hospital waiting rooms, bus and train stations, doorways, benches, parking garages, both on and under porches, on the curb, and under bridges. Some tried "DSS-ing it," or calling the Department of Social Services after hours with different names to secure emergency housing, and all had used several of the thousands of abandoned houses in Rochester. These last were by far their most frequent place to secure shelter, with a number of women saying there were "people out there who knew how to hook up electric or get heat" in these buildings. "Going into a rehab" also was an option for some of the women. All had great familiarity with the rehabilitation system and its resources in the community, with most having lost count of the number of times they had sought drug treatment; however, a common expression heard among these women was that "jail had replaced rehab—it was easier, you get all your needs met, even though withdrawal's hell."

It is not surprising that the winter months were most dreaded by the women. Many said they "worked so hard to get caught" during this time, but they could "never find a cop on the streets during a blizzard." Kristin, a 47-year-old heroin-addicted woman with AIDS, spoke of many winter nights huddled in doorways when some "kind soul" or "compassionate stranger" in the neighborhood where she worked would pick her up and just drive around, keeping her warm and getting her something to eat. Many women mentioned bar owners who had let them in after closing, as long they respected the establishment during business hours by keeping their distance from its customers, doors, and parking lots.

For many of the women, seeking shelter with people met through stays in jail or rehabilitation centers was very common. Most had done so, and some, such as the women in the Lives of Loss and Trauma group, described how they not only stayed together but also worked together, doing whatever hustle they were active in at the time. For prostitutes, in particular, the most frequently mentioned "homes" were the several hotels bordering the district where they worked, which had exceptionally low hourly and daily rates, as well as the houses of dates and friends, where tricking and sleeping could be done for $10 to $40 a night.

There also were common practices and places that the women used to take care of their day-to-day needs and obtain food while on the street. Judy expressed it well when she said, "The streets are my living room, bedroom, and front porch. The bodegas, they're my kitchen and refrigerator, and the Laundromat, bus station, or off-track betting parlor, that's my bathroom." Although personal needs and food were low on the list of each woman's priorities, they all spoke of the many "friendly" establishments in "the hood" where they could "stop for a minute" to take care of both. These included both charitable organizations, such as one church-based soup kitchen that also provided clothing, which all of the women said they frequented, as well as small neighborhood businesses.

The corner stores, or "bodegas" as Judy and others called them, were particularly useful for this purpose and had an almost symbiotic relationship with people like these women who were on the street. Not only did they buy the women's stolen wares, but they also serviced their individual needs for the single first cigarette of the day; a slice of pizza; flavored papers for their blunts; other drug paraphernalia, often weakly disguised as something else (e.g., a glass stem displayed as a small vase holding a flower); and the daily scratch-off lottery tickets, which seemed as addicting to the women as their drugs.

Highest on the list of these women's daily—or, more accurately, hourly—priorities were their drugs. Availability was absolutely no problem. All of the women spoke of the many drug houses located in the areas where they "lived" and the early morning traffic to and from them for the first hit or "blow." Also, as stated, the women all preferred to deal with known houses and not corner spots, which they were less likely to trust for quality or to use because a credited first hit was rarely possible. These drug houses, like the bodegas, also had a symbiotic relationship with the women.

Each woman's business was predictable, and each had a known credit score, whereby the risk of fronting the first hit was known. Prostitutes who partied with their dates brought additional sales, for which the women were usually compensated or tipped with a bag for themselves, and larcenists provided name-brand merchandise that was exchanged for a drug amount that equaled pennies on the dollar. As Donna remembered, "The things that come to your house when you sell are incredible. Anything you can possibly imagine." Also, although all of the women agreed that buying drugs was preferable to exchanging something of value for them, be it sex or property, they all also confessed that no one was above such bartering when desperate to get off E. "Nothing," Donna said, "becomes higher than addiction."

POLICE ENCOUNTERS

Two other more conventional institutions figured prominently in the lives of all the women in this study. The first was law enforcement, and for most of the women this meant the Rochester Police Department, and the second was the Monroe County Correctional Facility. With respect to the former, there was unfortunately a clear racial divide among the women in terms of their impressions of and claimed involvement with members of the Rochester Police Department, and this did not seem to be explained by either the nature of the offenses that the women committed or the area of town where they worked.

For example, among women who engaged in prostitution, Caucasian women were far more likely to report positive, and even helpful, experiences with law enforcement than African American or Hispanic women, regardless of where they picked up dates. Caucasian women said that they were often "warned off" by the police or "given breaks." As Debby, a Caucasian member of the Challenged group, recalled, "Most are okay. They give you a warning. I had this undercover guy pull up to me in the . . . parking lot. He walked up to me and asked, 'You know who I am?' I hauled outta there."

Caucasian women who were engaging in prostitution also reported that officers often stopped and told them about particular cars, men, or areas (including targeted drug houses) to avoid. Many also said they had cooperated with the police by providing information about people or places on the street, and several claimed they had dated and serviced cops. Tess, in particular, jokingly said she did not "discriminate when it came to customers" as she named several officers whom she said were her clients. Also, as stated, this association held true regardless of whether the woman worked in the area of Rochester known for prostitution or other more stable neighborhoods, like Elise did.

Elise would not work in the area of Rochester known for prostitution because it was "too violent." Instead, she walked the streets in a bordering, partially gentrified neighborhood that had more restaurants, bars, and commercial activity, as well as older large homes now converted into apartments. Elise said she knew most of the cops working this area and that they treated her "right, as long as I stay away from the places where people complain." A heroin addict, who said she's "replaced jail for rehab," Elise also claimed that she "watched where [she] did her drugs"; "nothing on the street," she said, "always in the car or back in the cut with the crackheads."

Caucasian larcenists and drug offenders also reported encounters with police that were, if not positive, at least accommodating or borderline respectful, civil ones. Most said, "There are some good ones, who calm you down and talk to you like a human being."

In contrast, among African American and Hispanic women, the most frequently heard expression was "I don't have nothing to do with no police," and that included the deputies in the jail. Regardless of the offenses these women committed, most said their arrests or treatment by the police had been "degrading," "bad," "nasty," or "rough." Shasta, for instance, who boosted and sold drugs, claimed that "all cops look at you like you use drugs or are a prostitute." Sabra likewise said it was a "no win with the police—they're assholes, they treat you like you're nothing." Marie claimed even worse, saying she knew many cops on the street who bought drugs or would "let you go if you showed them [something]." Cindy, who engaged in prostitution, just said they were "bad; they spray you with Mace, then beat you to the ground." Janie, a Hispanic booster now trying to sell drugs, called all her encounters with the police "nasty. They don't have to treat you the way they do. Hand-cuffing you in the store." Karla, also a booster, claimed even harsher treatment. "I keeps away from the police. They're pigs. I was pregnant— they maced me, got me on the ground, and put their knees in my back. And he was Black."

JAIL STAYS

As stated earlier, another institution that figured prominently in the lives of these women was the jail. In his groundbreaking and still-unrivaled work, *The Jail: Managing the Underclass in American Society*, John Irwin (1975) characterized the typical American jail as being a "meeting house" where marginal members of society who know each other reconnect; a "convalescent center" where these same marginal people can be cared for and rest; and a social institution, the latent function of which is to maintain or prepare marginal individuals for a "rabble existence" (p. 85). Irwin's insightful observations have great relevance to this study, and I elaborate on them and contextualize them further in the next chapter. However, for the purpose of this presentation of findings, they are highlighted here to provide a framework for discussion.

For the women interviewed in this research, jail—or, more accurately, repeated jail stays—did in fact serve the manifest function of social control, but these stays also had more latent functions, some of which did operate in the contradictory fashion first discussed by Irwin (1975). For instance, whereas on the one hand, the women's frequent trips to jail had typically resulted in many significant losses, both directly and indirectly, which appeared to ensure their continued rabble existence, on the other hand, these trips to jail also, as most of the women said, enabled them to survive at least for the time they were there, by "getting clean" and providing an environment in which much-needed food, rest, and medical care were possible.

The material and personal losses associated with frequent jail stays were many and varied. Rooms and apartments were lost, as were whatever personal belongings the women had managed to retain. Furniture, clothing, and personal items, such as photographs and papers of identity, were placed on the street like garbage, if not distributed among or held by friends. Even if a woman's possessions were held by others, safe retention was always an issue, with many women reporting the use or sale of possessions, money, or benefit cards by friends. Jail stays also interrupted and ultimately eradicated whatever progress a woman may have been making to get off the street. Treatment slots were lost, as were beds in transitional housing or benefit applications being processed. In addition, although most of the women had already informally placed children with relatives or agencies, their presence once again in jail often resulted in the final, formal loss of custody.

As stated, however, jail did provide what was a healthy stop or resting place for many. Jen said, "jail saved my life," and Cora claimed it was "a blessing. I got to the point where I didn't know if I was going to wake up." Pearl called it "three hots [hot meals] and a cot" and, like Elise, said it was a place that had "replaced" her many times in rehabilitation. Elise also said it was "the only time" she was healthy. She and many others also described jail by saying, "Unfortunately, I feel like it's home. I'm good here, eating, healthy, clean, got glasses—I even have a little bit of a job." When asked about negative impacts, Elise said, "I can't really think of any. None. Well, I guess I don't get to do what I want I want to do, but that's usually wrong anyway. I haven't lost anything, because I never had anything to lose." The easiest thing about being in jail, which she said was far more comfortable than her street existence, was having "everything done for you. A girl washes our socks and puts a happy face in with the laundry bag."

For a few women, jail stays also resulted in personal accomplishments, from obtaining a General Educational Development diploma; to visiting with a mother not seen since the woman entered street life; or communicating with one's children in a positive, clear-minded fashion. Several of the women expressed genuine pride at being trusted to perform "little jobs" while incarcerated, whether it was managing supplies for the unit or having responsibility over the women's meal trays. A handful also were able to use resources in the jail for obtaining and actually going to subsequent transitional placements after release.

Although these physical aspects of the jail stay were indeed positive, or at least helpful, for many of the women in this study, there was another, more consuming facet to the jail experience that was far less remedial and, in fact, by closely mirroring the values and norms of the street, as well as their resulting interpersonal dynamics, could be said to be nothing more than an extension and perhaps even a reinforcement of the women's outside street or rabble existence. For nearly all the women, jail was, as Irwin (1975) observed, a meeting house, and the experience itself was based on familiarity, not only with the physical structure and routine but also with the people who stayed and worked there. The women knew each other from the street or, as Elise said, "I see more of Mahogany in here than I do out there," and they knew each other's partners, friends, associates, and families. Kimber likewise pointed to several women, saying, "She, she, and she—we used to smoke together." Cindy claimed to "know everyone here—couple of faces, they're here all the time," and Sissy said, "You find out more information here than on the streets. People coming and going. Everyone knows somebody through drugs, who [had sex with] who's man, who's pregnant." As Ann summed it up, "We all got mutual friends and dealers, men we know, who's doing who."

The women also were familiar with each other's licks or scams. Many bought their drugs from Kay; everyone spoke of Jen's reputation as the best booster in Rochester; and, among the women who engaged in prostitution, Tess's repeated victimization by her pimp was a daily topic of conversation. For some women, such as Sherry and Darla, this familiarity was less than welcoming. As stated earlier, Sherry had her arm broken within minutes of arriving in the facility by a woman with whom she had a conflict on the outside, and all the women warned each other when Darla, a known thief, walked in. In addition to a great deal of personal familiarity in the unit, there was, according to nearly all the women, a "streetwise" attitude in jail. As Doris said, "I thought you heard a lot on the outside. In here, they talk to you like they're out there—on the street."

This streetwise attitude was manifested in a number of different norms and behaviors adhered to and displayed by the women. Primary among them was "boastin' and braggin'," which were the main talking activities among the women on a daily basis. Susan claimed that this was "all about competition—who's got the most commissary [items], who's got the biggest house." Sabra agreed, saying that "people-wise, jail was the street. They do stuff like people on the street—they gossip, play cards, talk about what they got."

Others said the boasting was more of an attempt to accomplish another lick, and that was either to get over on someone or to look and act tough. Kimber said it was "all a street game, doing whatever you can do to get something." Donna agreed, saying jail was "all street—a very small number of people trying to work on something. You gotta keep up on what's going on—talk the spot—who's using what, where, when, and how. Who's doing who." Everyone knew, for instance, that Jen's parents took care of her while she was in jail, dropping a good amount of money in her commissary account each week. Because of this, she ran the unit's "store," or fronted people commissary items for which she received a "two-for-one return," something Jen was not above boasting about. The women also knew that Chantell had an arrangement with a woman who was doing a weekend sentence to bring drugs into the unit on a weekly basis. Unfortunately for Chantell, this knowledge, shared with others to get something in return, usually in the form of commissary items, became a bit too widely known and resulted in her receiving a disciplinary infraction and stay "in the box [in disciplinary segregation]."

As stated earlier, boastful talk was also seen by the women as an inmate's attempt to look or act tough or for self-protection. Marie spoke of all the "war stories" that circulated among the women and how so many "punks" claimed that they had done "this or that to that woman over there or her man." Saying jail was "not a place to relax," Ann said, "[you] had to learn how to survive in here." "Someone's always tryin' to get somethin' outta you and you can't fight to the bloody end [like you would on the street]. You can't get punked in here. You gotta be smart, have the words, stand up." Esther, well known by both inmates and staff, as well as by me from a previous study, was particularly resourceful at demonstrating her toughness, which also bordered on intentional "craziness" or danger through regular nightly "plays" of her exploits and cunning on the street.

Although toughness, or at least readiness "to post up" (i.e., stand one's ground) figured prominently in the women's talk, drugs were the main topic of conversation among the inmates. There was agreement by the women that drugs figured into discussions in one of two ways. Some, a minority of the population, spent their days talking about how this time they were going to this or that place to stay clean. The majority, or according to Sabra, "those who didn't lie," spoke about "where they'll go and what they'll do to get drugs." Many made promises, that were not believed, that they would "hook up" when they got out and talked about the "first, second, and third thing" they would do, all of which involved drugs. Names and locations of known dealers were shared, as were people, spots, and areas of town to avoid. Also, all of the women were particularly resentful of another inmate, a pregnant heroin addict who was being maintained on methadone, which is jail policy so as to prevent miscarriage or harm to the fetus. Her name came up frequently during interviews, not out of disdain for using drugs while pregnant but because she was able to use and had such ready, approved access to what everyone else wanted.

CONCLUDING REMARKS

Because of their addictions, the majority of the women in this study had become street women: Their lives were of the street and on the street. In this chapter I have provided a glimpse into that world and examined the norms, means, arrangements, and institutions of it that affected each individual's daily survival. These women remained hustlers and spoke with pride of how their street smarts enabled them to survive, at least marginally. They talked about the people and places in their communities that provided safety, sustenance, shelter, and the drugs they needed to stay "healthy." In many respects, their interchanges with these entities were almost symbiotic in nature, with each deriving some benefit from the other. This was especially true for the local licit and illicit businesses where they lived and worked.

The roles played by law enforcement officials in the women's daily survival also were highlighted. It was, however, the jail and the women's repeated stays in it that were probably the most influential institution in "maintaining" these women. The jail exerted this influence on the women not only in a beneficial way, by providing them a brief respite from the street, a place where they could get momentarily healthy and sober, but it also had a far less benign influence on them, because it was, in its lifestyle, values, and norms, nothing more than a reflection and extension of the street, where the outlook and behaviors associated with hustling or catching a good lick were necessary for survival and thus reinforced among the women, both individually and collectively.

Discussion, Conclusions, and Implications

In chapter 3, I discussed the research interests that directed my inquiry and introduced three concepts that I said would become closely aligned with them. These concepts—hustling trajectories, hustling outlooks, and hustling lifestyles—typically have not been applied to the women of this study, because they imply far too much agency, wits, and even sharpness than is generally allotted women who engage in street crime. In advancing the concepts it was not my intent to romanticize these women or the wretched lives they eventually lead. Instead, my aim, quite simply, was to present what they had to say about themselves, their pasts and presents, as women hustling to survive in the marginal world of the street. It is now my task, in this last chapter, to discuss or make sense of what I have learned about that life and to do so using, to the greatest extent possible, the women's own voices and thoughts. Once this is completed, I highlight suggestions for future or continued study.

ENTRY INTO CRIMINALITY: THE HUSTLING TRAJECTORY

On the basis of my research and that of many others, I believe it is safe to say that childhood victimization has a great deal to do with women becoming involved in crime. My understanding of this connection, however, is somewhat different and a bit more complicated than that advanced in some of the literature. Although nearly all the women in this study had suffered horrific pasts, marred by years of familial abuse, neglect, instability, and deviance, they certainly were not constituted by and explained solely in terms of their status as victims; neither were they leading any revolution with respect to drugs and crime on the streets of Rochester. Instead, they were individuals for whom victimization had meant different things; they also were individuals with varied personal resources who looked at and reacted to particular social situations differently. Moreover, because of these individual distinctions they also seemed to attach very different meanings to and derive varied feelings from their involvements in hustling and crime.

Thus, my interpretation of the victimization-to-crime trajectory is neither linear nor uniform. It does not begin with abuse, progress through drugs, and end in crime that is solely drug related. It also does not assume application to all or most women offenders. Instead, my rendering of this pathway places more weight on the perceptual processes of the individual and how these were shaped not only by a history of victimization but also by personal resources and particular social situations. In other words, I found that the women's specific hustling trajectories varied depending on the influence and interaction of these several factors. Similarly, hustling appeared to mean very different things, based on the distinct effects of these forces, for each of the six pathways to crime that I identified.

My results, then, present somewhat of a challenge to the typical victimization-to-crime trajectory and its underlying assumptions about women's lack of agency and volition. They also question the implicit thinking that drug use precedes women's criminality and determines the course of illicit activities pursued. In fact, very few of the women I talked to expressly linked their offense histories or drug use to the past harms that caused them, and even fewer said they became involved in crime solely for the purpose of supporting addictions foisted on them by prior victimization or by the men in their lives.

Instead, for the majority of women in this study the pathway to crime seemed to result not so much from a push trajectory into illicit activity based on need, be it personal or physical, but more from a pull or lure into the lifestyle that they saw crime offering them. The task of interpretation and theorizing, then, becomes to detail and understand what underlay this perception and influenced the women to pursue a lifestyle of petty crimes such as theft, prostitution, and drug sales.

I argue here that what many of these women initially sought through crime and their relationships on the street was not an escape or an attempt to self-medicate through that life but more of an effort to gain and demonstrate that which had been denied, yet required, of them as children by dysfunctional families and neighborhoods infested with crime and violence. What these women sought was a sense of self-efficacy or mastery of their fate, including both the mindset or attitude that they were survivors or capable of what was expected to succeed in particular situations or environments and that they possessed the requisite skill sets to do so (see Bandura, 1997; Gecas, 1989). For other women, especially those who had suffered the most loss and trauma in their lives, street behaviors and hustles were less an expression of individual efficacy and power and more an indication of the deep and pervasive psychic harm caused by highly dysfunctional home lives.

Thus, to understand most of these women's pathways into crime it is necessary to place them within the context of their families, in which they were either withheld the upbringing necessary to feel self-efficacious or just the opposite, lived in more privileged or nurturing familial settings and developed high aspirations that were subsequently dashed by negative educational and employment experiences. It also is necessary to locate this motivation for self-efficacy within the early neighborhood environments of the women, because it was there that the demonstration of personal resources and skills such as smarts, strength, and control were required for daily survival. Such a multilevel focus also is needed to understand women whose entry into crime reflected differing psychic influences.

In the discussion that follows, I examine my six hustling trajectories with the preceding comments in mind. More specifically, I look at each trajectory for the relative contributions of the three factors highlighted earlier: (a) victimization history, (b) personal resources, and (c) social forces. The meaning of hustling for each group also is discussed in terms of its place in the women's personal narratives and its role in either enhancing feelings of self-efficacy or expressing deeper psychological issues.

I use the expression *self-narrative* or *personal narrative* in the manner suggested by Maruna (2001), who argued that such constructions not only provide a person with a "cognitive schema" or "information-processing structure," by which he or she attaches meaning to others in the environment, but also enable that person to define and understand him- or herself as an individual (p. 40). As Maruna explained,

> Essentially, people construct stories to account for what they do and why they do it. These narratives impose an order on people's actions and explain people's behaviors with a sequence of events that connect up to explanatory goals, motivations, and feelings. These self narratives then act to shape and guide future behavior, as people act in ways that agree with the stories or myths they have created about themselves. (p. 40)

All in the Family

When I discussed the family backgrounds of women in the All in the Family group, I highlighted their commonality of parental neglect and observed how most spoke of lost childhoods or the assumption of caregiving responsibilities for younger siblings while still children themselves. These women thus grew up fast, as they told me, because of the deviance or instability of parental figures. Also, they not only served as the mother figure for other brothers and sisters, but they also supported everyone in the household with their early and extensive work experiences. These were, in other words, not women who had been weakened by the neglect of their childhoods; instead, they were individuals who had developed certain resources to withstand and triumph over it. Primary among such resources were their hustling skills, outlook, and sense of self, all of which were learned and exercised within a family and community deeply entrenched in crime.

Because of this criminogenic context, the women in this group did not run from home to engage in street life, as E. Miller's (1986) earlier street women had; instead, they were schooled in that life by members of their families, and thus they more closely resembled the low-level women offenders profiled by recent researchers (Dunlap, 1992; Maher, Dunlap, & Johnson, 2006): "They learned about street culture within their [own] households . . .

[which] consisted of several often interchangeable adults whose primary economic activities included heroin, crack or other drugs sales and/or non-drug users' criminality" (Maher et al., 2006, p. 26). Also, given the role and primacy of this context, I argue that the mechanics by which these women were socialized to street life and culture clearly were those associated with social learning theory (Bandura, 1986) and its more recent construction, cognitive social learning theory (Meichenbaum, 1977).

Moreover, the street and its hustling outlook became normalized for the women and a critical part of their own identity or self-narrative. Thus, for these individuals hustling, and especially boosting, was "all [they] ever knew," and, because of this, it also was very much who and what they saw themselves as being, with each woman indeed claiming that she was "the best there ever was or would be."

Just Another Addiction

Family and community life also appeared operative in explaining the path to criminality for women in the Just Another Addiction group. However, for these individuals, both were perceived not as benign learning environments but as very dangerous entities that required the successful demonstration of "street smarts" to survive (Anderson, 1999). Parents were hustlers, addicted to drugs, or "running the streets," and other occupants of that venue were frequent visitors to childhood homes, where drama was a daily yet unpredictable presence. Moreover, unlike women in the All in the Family group, who had reminisced about past neighborhoods, calling them "bittersweet," the women in the Just Another Addiction group had nothing positive to say about the streets where they had lived: The bottom line for each was that their neighborhoods were "all about violence and drugs."

The impact of these distorted socializing forces on the women's feelings of self-efficacy and personal narratives was monumental, ultimately resulting in the defensive worldview I discussed in chapter 2. Growing up in violent homes in perilous communities, they struggled with feelings of vulnerability that were masked by "a willingness to use violence and intimidation to repel others" (Fleisher, 1995, p. 104). Such behaviors were in fact "survival skills" for these individuals, who trusted no one and felt "threatened by forces outside their control to protect themselves" (Fleisher, 1995, p. 105). Accordingly, they saw themselves as "bad girls" (Messerschmidt, 1997) and acted in the "ways of the badass" (Katz, 1988) so characteristic of life on the street, both as a means to be treated with "a certain deference and regard, which [translated] into a sense of physical and psychological control" (Anderson, 1999, p. 34).

Show Me the Money

Whereas the women in the Just Another Addiction group appeared to be motivated in their criminal pursuits by the sense of self-efficacy that success in that realm gave them, those in the Show Me the Money group had different reasons for their criminal activity. These reasons were rooted in far more stable, protective, and nurturing childhoods than those of other women in this study. For the Show Me the Money women crime was in essence nothing more than a means to an end: They stole or dealt drugs not to demonstrate toughness and street smarts but simply because they wanted "fast money" and had the skills to get it.

In many respects, the women of the Show Me the Money group clearly resembled Rachel and her upbringing, mentioned in chapter 2 of this volume and chronicled by Dunlap and Johnson (1996), as well as the women profiled by Denton and O'Malley (1999), Fagan (1994), Maxwell and Maxwell (2000), Mieczkowski (1994), and Morgan and Joe (1997). Like Rachel, they had the wherewithal, personal resources, or cunning to use legitimate jobs for the opportunities they presented to obtain cash illicitly and quickly. Also like Rachel, they had amassed great social (or criminal) capital through an early exposure to street life and its ways, means, and skills for making fast money, all of which were acquired within the context of a generally protective familial environment.

These women clearly had few problems with self-efficacy, grounded as they had been in a nurturing, safe home environment and positive school experiences (Bandura, 1986). Their personal narratives likewise spoke of nothing but success, and it was to demonstrate this with materialistic symbols that they hustled, selling drugs or dating dealers. These also were individuals who understood Katz's (1988) discussion about "earning and burning money" in the quest for high living. For them, appearance was indeed everything, providing as it did the "cultural apparatus" of the "good life" (Anderson, 1990, p. 242). Likewise, they certainly echoed Stephens's (1991) comments about the underlying purpose of a hedonistic lifestyle, where "money, clothes and cars are used for image management as much as for any intrinsic worth they may have" (p. 47). These were individuals, in other words, who engaged in conspicuous consumption not only to demonstrate their "cool transcendence over . . . financial concerns" but also to announce their own personal coolness or worth at having made it (Jacobs, 1999, p. 30). Also, much more than any other group, they indeed resembled the women of Anderson's (1999) "Baby Club," who sought status and demonstration of the good life among female peers through the appearance and things they provided their children.

Partiers by Trade

Women in the Partiers by Trade group also had a relatively early exposure to street life in the city of Rochester. However, for them this exposure came not within the context of a stable, supportive childhood but after an upbringing characterized by highly dysfunctional or absent relationships with parents and minimal, if any, aspirations for the self. In fact, these women, the majority of whom were Caucasian and working class, clearly demonstrated the "pushout or runaway without resources pathway" described by E. Miller (1986). Most had left home by their early teens because they felt unwanted, and when they did leave, the break with family was wide and deep, because family provided little or no further emotional and financial support.

Thus, without a net of human or social capital, these women used the only means they had, and to survive they did what they knew best: to hustle men with sex, first for money and then drugs (Tea, 2003). Whether dancing, stripping, or tending bar, the women scammed the men they entertained as "easy slays," telling one fake story after another, all the while becoming more and more involved in drugs and eventually unable to do anything more than prostitution to survive.

These individuals, who were impulsive and early risk-takers as adolescents, with few connections to their intentionally distant parents, showed all the marks of what Gottfredson and Hirschi (1990) stated results from poor child-rearing practices. Attached to no one in their childhood homes, they had few internal controls over what they did and to whom. With little interest in school, they left because they could, and what they ran to on the street was an arena for their constant partying, hanging at the bars, and "running the streets."

The early partying lifestyle of these women, modeled on that of their emotionally distant parents, clearly appears to have been related to the anger and depression they experienced in households where stress was always relieved with a drink (Droppleman & Wilt, 1993; Seabrook, 1993). Alcohol not only dulled the anger they felt toward rejecting parents but also served to enhance what little self-esteem these women had. Their subsequent partying life was anything but fun and consisted of daily attempts to feel good about themselves with drugs and their abilities to scam men. It was the latter, when it consisted of a good lick, that seemed to inflate the meager senses of self-respect these women had. Their many street survival skills, and their animated discussions of them, also appeared to lift them somewhat. Thus, although these women were lacking in legal self-efficacy, their sense of criminal self-efficacy (i.e., the skills and smarts that enabled them to survive the street at least somewhat successfully) was clearly intact and something they valued and put forth as their self-narrative (Agnew, 2006).

Challenged

Women in the Challenged group also were heavily involved in drugs and mainly engaged in prostitution to obtain money for drugs. It was they who most closely resembled the women in early pathways research. The primary themes that characterized their movement to the street, in other words, were those of victimization, running away, male initiation to drug use, self-medication, and what can only be called criminal desperation. However, even these women seemed motivated to obtain a sense of control in their lives, especially with respect to whatever disability they had, and unfortunately it was drug ingestion that seemed to accomplish this for them.

These women's childhood histories were deeply marred by repeated physical and sexual victimization, usually inflicted by caregivers or siblings. Most also had been "put out" by families to other relatives or institutions. Moreover, as a group, the women had typically been introduced to drugs by the people in their lives, primarily men with whom they were involved. They continued and escalated this use as a form of self-medication, saying the drugs made them feel normal, level, or less like a "knucklehead"; "unafraid"; "happy, in charge"; and like a "big girl."

In addition to prostitution, these women also engaged in minor criminal scams, which, like their drug use, also seemed to make them feel normal or better about themselves. As one woman, who functioned as a lookout for a crack house, told me, "At least I'm good at something." Although this sense of criminal self-efficacy appeared to be a motivation for engaging in petty criminal pursuits, it typically was spoken of in the context of other feelings the women experienced when committing minor crimes. These feelings consisted of the "sense of pleasant fearfulness, . . . [the] excitement, challenge, fun or adventure" the women derived from executing "good licks" (Lofland, 1969, p. 107). Indeed, they used words such as *adventure, fun, mission,* and *joyride* to describe their different hustles. It was clear that they enjoyed the "sneaky thrills" (Katz, 1988) of being daring or "making an excursion into the forbidden" (Lofland, 1969, p. 109), because by doing so they could be like anyone else and not "the dummies" they called themselves.

Lives of Loss and Trauma

In contrast to women in the Challenged group, who seemed to make their way onto the street to escape lives of failure and to feel normal, individuals in the Lives of Loss and Trauma group appeared to seek on the street that which they had lost or never had: a sense of self, safely rooted in family. Indeed, the backgrounds and early family lives of these women were far more damaging, both psychically and emotionally, than any other group in this study.

These women had experienced brutal physical and sexual abuse within their childhood homes and, because of the psychological or substance abuse problems of caregivers, felt neither secure nor wanted. Many spoke of "growing up on the frontline, fighting for [their lives]" and described themselves as nothing more than "shells" or "voids" who were told by family that they "should have been aborted" or that they would "be dead before 18." They also were more likely than others to have lost significant loved ones as children, which only heightened their sense of aloneness or being motherless. Coupled with this extreme rejection and individual loss, these women also said they "felt different" or "less stable" than their peers. They often had been labeled as "hard to manage" or as a "problem child in school" and felt like outcasts there, which they dealt with by running away and subsequently becoming officially labeled as different with an adjudication of Persons in Need of Supervision (Meares, 2000, p. 29).

The solutions the women fashioned to deal with their feelings were threefold. First, as just stated, they "ran to the street as soon as [they] could," which was far earlier than others in this study, and they did so often. Second, they "stayed high," as they said, "as much as [they] could," and thus they evinced a more extensive history with hard drugs than most of the other women. Third, they also connected with people like themselves on the street, boosting and living with friends made in rehabilitation centers or jail, who provided some sense of connectedness, predictability, and control over one's daily pursuits, which had been totally absent and impossible in their former worlds.

The early use by these women of "stimulus-seeking behaviour such as reckless sexuality, substance abuse, gambling, [and] even theft" (Meares, 2000, p. 56) clearly seems related to efforts aimed at dulling the intense pain associated with their "pervasive sense of emptiness" (Meares, 2000, p. 56). Moreover, with an extensive drug history and a deep inability to cope in situations of stress, anger, or threats to their relationships, the women of this group were like Daly's (1992) "harmed-and-harming" individuals: They lashed out and harmed others, for which they, unlike most of the women in this study, were charged with crimes against the person. In fact, theirs was very much a dog-eat-dog world in which no one, including the people with whom they lived and hustled, were cared for or trusted in any way.

Thus, the emotional damage done to these women as children certainly resulted in their having a defensive worldview (Fleisher, 1995).

More important, however, is that it also left them with a great deal of debilitating shame and anger that were deeply enduring and highly recursive in their lives (Scheff, 1990). This feeling trap of *shame-rage,* as Scheff (1990) called it, although implanted by the women's early lack of healthy connections to caretakers, continued to play out and influence all subsequent interactions and relationships. Their lives, in other words, consisted of emotional roller coasters that replayed the rejection they had experienced as children: Any hint of disapproval or rebuff in a relationship brought back childhood shame and anger, which led to further rejection, and so on. Also, unlike the members of other groups, the self-narratives these women presented were constructed totally in terms of past harms: They were, as they told me, "damaged goods."

WOMEN AS OFFENDERS: THE HUSTLING OUTLOOK

Just as the women in this study differed in terms of the paths they had taken to the street, they also evinced variety in the crimes they committed there. With few exceptions, in other words, these individuals were not one thing as opposed to another. They were neither boosters, prostitutes, nor drug sellers, exclusively: Instead, they were true hustlers who did what they did on the basis of particular skill sets and their perception of an apparent opportunity at a particular time. The research conducted for this book thus challenges what have been the prevailing thoughts about women's extended involvement in low-level crime, that it is typically male initiated and drug related, as well as insensible and pathetic, limited solely to street-level sex work.

The criminal careers of these Rochester street women suggest otherwise, and they highlight the need for both research and theory to examine women's criminality in a temporal sense, in terms of where a woman actually is in her career, as well as contextually or functionally, within the criminal world of which she is a part. Furthermore, the women's crimes seemed, at least initially, to say something about their motivations as well as their self-perceptions. These attributions also were present in how they described the commission of particular offenses or the norms they observed in carrying out their hustles.

In the discussion that follows, I examine each group in terms of these dimensions. Accordingly, I detail what appear to be underlying motivational aspects to the women's offenses, and I place their crimes within the criminal opportunity structures of the communities where they lived and worked. Normative practices associated with specific hustles also are highlighted, as is the nature of each group's criminality over time.

Women in the All in the Family group began their hustling activity by boosting. As I have stated in previous chapters, boosting for them was very much a social thing, both as children when they shopped with friends and family and as young adults when they showed off and plied their wares in the clubs of Rochester. These women initially saw themselves as true hustlers, living and loving the fast life with their wits and skills. Their boosting activities were well planned and executed, with stores targeted for permeability, times chosen for unfettered access, items selected for subsequent salability, and an appearance presented by the woman as just another shopper of substance.

As the women of this group became more and more involved in the fast life of drinking and using drugs, their well-honed skills were compromised, their rationality became clouded, their shopping lost its excitement, and their appearance deteriorated to that of a "drug fiend." Some continued with other types of theft where these personal qualities were less important, and others just panhandled or engaged in prostitution on the streets that had once been their marketplace.

Women in the Partiers by Trade group also began their hustling of men as a social thing, working either the strip clubs of Rochester, its afterhours gambling joints, or other somewhat shady social clubs. Immersed in this partying lifestyle of drugs and men, they grew old fast and quickly had to resort to catching their licks on the streets of neighborhoods in northwest Rochester known for prostitution.

Numerous norms directed how they worked these streets, with many qualities defining the good lick they all sought as well as the bad lick they avoided. Certain locations were preferred, such as bus stops for the camouflage they allowed from law enforcement and parking lots for both their visibility and access to customer traffic. Other locations, such as parks and crack houses, were shunned because of their potential for danger. The women similarly had shared understandings about what constituted a good trick as opposed to a bad one. Unfortunately, however, most were at the point in their addictions where much of this rational thinking was no longer possible, and thus all of the women reported numerous victimizations on the street. All also indicated that they did far more than hooking with their dates and often "viced" them for money, credit cards, cars, or drugs. It was these activities that now seemed to explain their more frequent trips to jail.

Women in the Show Me the Money group were all about living the good life of fast (easy) cash, the latest fashions, and any material possession that spoke to their having "made it." These women wanted only the best for themselves, and they wanted it quickly, as a demonstration of their sharp wits and personal resources. Accordingly, they did not boost, because for that they would have to unload stolen goods, but they executed a variety of cash scams, stealing from jobs or engaging in credit card and identity thefts.

Because of their skills and the control they had over personal use, these women also were more likely to sell drugs, seeing themselves as "smarter than the men." Most had developed arrangements with others in the drug economy where they were able to rent rooms for selling drugs or secure a spot for selling in rural towns outside of Rochester. The women in this group were the youngest in my study, and for this reason, as well as because of their unique personal resources perhaps, they had not progressed as deeply as others into addiction. They thus continued to move easily, frequently, and with great rationality among their different licks for generating cash.

The criminality of the Challenged group was a sharp reflection of the women's desperate search for drugs and vulnerability to victimization on the streets of Rochester. Unlike others, they were more likely to engage in sex for crack and to do so in the city's many crack houses, where they were either victimized or arrested. These women also incurred charges that resulted from being used by others to hold stolen property, for example, or to serve as a lookout for some dealer in exchange for a dime bag of crack. Their state of mind also influenced behaviors that brought them to the attention of law enforcement officers. They, more than others, for instance, were less crafty and evasive with their crimes: Because of an intense need for drugs, they often smoked in areas visible to the police and, when trying to secure money through dates or panhandling, they frequently appeared "off the hook" and disorderly.

The initial lick for most women in the Just Another Addiction group was boosting. Although many of the norms and behaviors that directed their shopping were similar to those of women in the other groups, others were quite different. For instance, for these women stealing was not a social event, as it was for the All in the Family group; neither was it about getting quick cash, as it had been for those in the Show Me the Money group. Instead, they boosted, at least initially, solely because of the euphoria and self-esteem they experienced while doing it. For them, boosting had been "an art" or "incredible," and this included both the theft itself and the marketing of goods afterward throughout their neighborhoods, with the area's drug dealers being their best customers for the latest brand-name items. Other women in this group began their criminality by selling drugs, which they described using the same euphoric language of those who stole, saying it was "beautiful" and "better than going to the clubs."

What became of the women in this group over time also speaks to the addictive qualities they attributed to their crimes. With their growing dependency on drugs, most ended up in prostitution-related activity; however, they, unlike others, were often lured back to boosting, even though they knew their appearance betrayed them, and the time they spent in jail on these charges continued to take a toll.

As I have mentioned several times in this book, the women in the Lives of Loss and Trauma group were the most damaged of all in my study, and this was clearly reflected in the nature and patterns of their criminal activity. What appeared to distinguish them as offenders initially was the tremendous variety of their first arrests. In particular, unlike other women in the study, these women were more likely to have violent crimes against persons in their histories as they lashed out uncontrollably in response to the pain of their pasts. Their histories also revealed an almost frenzied movement among offenses, in both diversity and volume. This movement seemed predicated not on rationality or the criminal opportunities of the street but more on where the women were emotionally at the time and the whims of others with whom they were involved.

Thus, these women continued to commit crimes against persons, and they seemed to take far more risks, exercising little thought, in what they did offense wise. They also, unlike other women in this study, were more likely to have committed crimes with "friends" met on the street, in jail, or a drug treatment facility. The women, likewise, were more likely to attribute everything they did on the street to the pain caused them in their pasts.

Finally, it should be noted that nearly all of the women in the study claimed to have sold drugs in some manner or intermittently for at least "a minute" while criminally active. This included both those who mainly committed property offenses as well as women primarily engaged in prostitution. Also, for most of these women, selling drugs was not a distinct one-time activity that occurred as some separate phase of the woman's career; instead, it was something that was done throughout their criminal involvement, in one form or another, when the opportunity presented itself. The patterns of this activity, in other words, were as varied as the women's own criminality. Some worked with male or female partners, others were paid for working shifts in drug houses, several rented and sold from rooms in the homes of known users, and many provided the money and credentials for a dealer to secure property from which to sell.

Thus, although patterns and timing may have varied, there was a common theme to the women's involvement in drug sales, and that was that selling was an integral part of, or actually made possible by, the lifestyle associated with their other criminal activities. In the case of boosters, for instance, the most frequently named customer of stolen merchandise was the drug dealers, all of whom were said to be very materialistic, valuing the name-brand clothing and items stolen by the women. Many recalled how it was this sales connection that led to the opportunity to diversify one's criminality through the selling of drugs. Similar opportunities were presented to women primarily engaged in prostitution, most of whom also copped drugs for their dates.

SURVIVING THE STREET AND JAIL: THE HUSTLING LIFESTYLE

Just as crime was about a good lick or hustle to the street women of this study, so too was their survival while so engaged. Also, like their various offenses, the women's patterns of living both on the street and in the jail were very much influenced by their particular skill level and especially their ability to access and negotiate opportunity structures within that community, both legal and illegal. Although most of the women had long since lost what limited familial resources they once had, they were not without the personal and interpersonal cunning necessary to stay safe and "off E" in their daily lives. What facilitated this was an acute sense of street smarts, which all of the women displayed, and an extensive familiarity with the numerous norms and institutionalized hustles of street life in Rochester.

The women in the study were, for instance, keenly aware of people and places to avoid and generally did so unless dope sick, which most of them claimed they managed by having an established and symbiotic credit relationship with known dealers. Also, all said that beds and showers could accessed through drug-using associates, as long as money or drugs were in hand. If the women lacked money or drugs, other opportunities were sought, including dates who thought they would "get more" if a motel room were obtained and, in rare cases, compassionate strangers or the occasional bar owner who provided a brief respite from the street after hours. For most of the women, however, protection from the elements came not in the form of people but through their own personal resources to "just keep walking" or to find shelter in a variety of marginal venues, be they doorways, abandoned houses, parking garages, or hospital waiting rooms.

In addition to these physical structures were the community resources the women accessed to survive, and these resources stood in an almost symbiotic relationship with the women in terms of their own economic viability. As described in chapter 3, it was from the many corner stores in the ghettoes of Rochester that the women obtained their basic necessities, including loosies, drug paraphernalia, scratch-off lottery tickets, and the occasional slice of pizza. It was at these same locations, as well as other establishments in their neighborhoods (i.e., wherever there were people), that the women fenced or sold their stolen goods and committed various forms of fraud.

Survival in jail required a similar level of street smarts and resourcefulness, but in this case the norms that applied included staying on top of the scams of others to avoid being "punked" or "gotten over," boasting and bragging about one's toughness to maintain personal safety, and being aware of who got what in commissary and could be conned with acts of friendship or sex for merchandise. Life in the jail, in other words, closely mirrored that of the street and consisted, as Irwin (1975) argued, of little more than a preparation for a continued rabble existence.

The women displayed, for example, "the mentality or outlook needed for [such an] existence" (Irwin, 1975, p. 87), and this was reinforced in their daily interactions with staff and each other. Nobody trusted anyone, and there was a wariness, a caution, not only about people but also about potentially dangerous situations. For instance, although women who knew each other from the street appeared to sit together as friends when playing cards or watching television, they all expressed during their interviews that "you have no friends in jail—just associates, people you use with on the street." The women also seemed to know when a fight was going to happen, whom it would involve, and what was behind the altercation.

Irwin (1975) called this attitude of opportunism, or being "alert to opportunities for personal gain" (p. 88) another aspect of the rabble mentality. In fact, one of the most common expressions I heard from the women about their stays in jail was the maxim that one had to be "gay for the stay and Muslim for the tray" (i.e., exchange sex for commissary items and claim Islam as one's religious affiliation to obtain better meals). The women also clearly demonstrated two other facets of the rabble mentality reinforced by jail life according to Irwin: (a) the spirit of making do and (b) improvisation.

Many of the women slept as long as they could each day to make time go faster. Others pled for any kind of job just to pass the time, and most wanted to attend the limited programmatic activities available for women, which consisted mainly of volunteer Bible study and self-help groups. Writing letters, some of which were never sent, and journaling also were engaged in, if the woman had money to obtain paper. Braiding and doing hair were regular pastimes, and on one occasion I learned of a play staged by an inmate (known as "the brother" in the unit) about her life and exploits on the street, which everyone talked about for days. However, the two main activities or ways of making do in the jail were talking and watching television. Life for these women was a very passive existence: Very few received visits, and even fewer were able to place collect calls to friends or family on the street.

In the midst of this passivity and making do, however, the women also displayed what Irwin (1975) called a spirit of improvisation. Several had a regular fitness routine, which involved walking briskly for an extended time around the day space of the unit. Makeup was fashioned out of pencils, crayons, and dried Kool-Aid, and uniforms were altered, where possible, to appear less baggy and more "fashionable." Food was saved or bartered, and cups that had held instant soup purchased through commissary were a valued possession, used throughout the woman's stay as her sole drinking receptacle.

Events and behaviors that demonstrated the role of jail stays in the women's cultural and social preparation for a continued rabble existence were noted and discussed in chapter 7. These included the many personal and material losses incurred because of frequent jail stays as well as the nature of the women's interactions while incarcerated. The latter included not only the topics of conversations, which were either street or drug related, but also the manner in which the women verbally engaged each other through boasting and bragging, which I saw, ironically, as just another attempt to catch a good lick.

CONCLUSIONS AND IMPLICATIONS FOR FUTURE RESEARCH

The criminological literature on women and crime generally starts from the assumption that histories of abuse and victimization are implicated in women's entry to crime and that therefore the goal of theorizing should be to fill the "black box" between these common pasts and subsequent criminal involvement (Daly, 1992). This is the first theme of the literature. How this is done reflects the second theme of the literature: to posit minimal agency or volition on the woman's part, as she appears driven into crime by her need for drugs, used to self-medicate the trauma of victimization, or her quest for normal romantic and familial relationships dictated by gender but never experienced in life. She thus becomes represented not as an offender but as a victim turned survivor through a life of crime, which is the third theme in the literature (Daly, 1992).

The research I conducted for this book suggests that there are several ways to fill the black box between victimization and crime and that there is a continuum with respect to agency as well as a variety of hustling modalities engaged in by women on the street. Thus, it is much more in line with and adds to the understanding provided by more recent research (Denton & O'Malley, 1999, 2006; Dunlap & Johnson, 1996; Maher, 1997; Maher et al., 2006).

On some levels, my study appears to confirm the observations of researchers that a woman's early involvement in selling drugs seems to protect her from a future in prostitution. Fagan (1994), for one, argued that this protection or insulation is rooted primarily in the income a person garners from drug sales. My research suggests that what seems to be more important in this scenario than income are the individual skills and abilities necessary to generate and sustain it. These are the personal resources and qualities that the women have both to control their own drug use and to function as a skillful businesswoman in what appears to be a drug scene still dominated by men.

Nearly every woman in this study claimed to have sold drugs at some point in her criminal career. When asked why they had stopped, all repeated an often-heard maxim: that users simply could not use and sell. This was not simply because they smoked up their profit; even more important was the fact that buyers did not trust sellers who were users, believing that they always dipped into the bags they sold to skim off drugs for their own personal use. It was clear, in this research, at least, that the maxim was quite true. The few successful dealers I interviewed did indeed control their personal use of drugs or claimed not to use at all.

However, these women also had other qualities that distinguished them as individuals from the larger subject population of my study. These women had a more stable background that resulted in the acquisition of a high level of human capital and skills, they very much resembled Rachel, as stated earlier, the crack dealer described by Dunlap and Johnson (1996). They also displayed, however, a very gendered (and resourceful) way of selling drugs. Kay, for example, sat on the block with her children and female friends, who were pregnant like she. "Who's gonna bother a pregnant lady and her kids?" she asked. Kay also made only small sales, leaving the weight (and the risk) to her husband, saying, "He's a man—let him drive around." Moreover, Kay sold primarily to other women, many of whom were now were sitting with her in jail. Male customers were just far too risky, she said, and were more likely to try and rob or hurt you. Kay knew of what she spoke: She had been robbed four times before she modified her market base.

Sassy similarly reported the value of gender in her selling career, saying, "We're smarter. Mens are dumb. I stand right there with it in my hands. Police aren't gonna mess with me, dressed pretty, in heels. I'm talking to him because it's my baby's father. No problem. I'll leave officer." Sassy summed it up by saying, "It's like Adam and Eve—we can persuade the police. They won't mess with you." An alternative gendered approach to drug sales was seen in Janie, a former booster who said, "women is taking over" in the drug business. Janie lived off the proceeds of sex work, not because she pimped or engaged in prostitution but because she hustled drugs for women on the street and their dates. She also claimed that she watched out for "the hos," like a "real pimp's supposed to do, but doesn't anymore."

As reported earlier, many of the women also said that although they would not sell drugs within the city limits of Rochester because of the dangers posed by male competition, they had no problem traveling to the suburbs and rural towns of the county for this purpose. Not only did they feel superior or smarter than their customers in these areas, but they also were able to overcharge them by city standards. These gender-structured behaviors for selling drugs displayed by Kay and others clearly present a subject for further inquiry and research.

Also suggested for additional research is a related question into which I had hoped to gain some insight with this study, but instead was left with contradictory findings. Has the role of women changed in the current drug market scene? My sample was fairly evenly divided on this issue. Some of the women said yes, "we're moving up—who would you rather buy from—a woman or some punk kid on the corner?" In contrast, others adamantly claimed that women just did not have the presence or toughness to compete successfully in the market and still remained in low-level ancillary roles, renting apartments for dealers, acting as mules (i.e., drug carriers) or lookouts, or doing shifts in drug houses. What was interesting and fairly unanimous, however, was that so many women aspired to this career path and, when possible, engaged in so many novel and resourceful hustles related to it.

This research also highlights the importance of examining individual criminal activity within the community context in which it occurs. Although the crimes these women committed definitely were influenced by where they were as individuals in terms of personal drug use, offenses also were very much shaped by the criminal opportunities presented by both the people and the institutions in their immediate environment. Drug dealers figured prominently in the lives of boosters and prostitutes alike, with the former servicing them with valued goods and the latter constituting a market base consisting of their own personal use and that of dates who wanted to party.

Other members of this informal economic sector, such as independent contractors and individuals who frequented gambling joints and after-hours clubs, also were important to these women's criminality and street survival. So too were the police; however, in this case there was a clear racial divide among the women. Whereas Caucasian women who engaged in prostitution had what amounted to a working relationship with law enforcement officers in receiving or providing information, African American and Hispanic women claimed racist, brutal treatment by Rochester police. The importance of examining the interplay of all these community-level actors in the criminality of low-level women offenders cannot be overstated and should be the focus of future research.

Included in this group of actors are the significant others, both male and female, with whom the women associated. As reported, the individuals from one group in this study, the women in the Lives of Loss and Trauma group, did not act alone in committing crime. Instead, they worked with associates, male and female, whom they had met on the street, in rehab, or in jail, to catch a good lick, which was primarily boosting. Such collective activity in crime beyond that of boyfriends and spouses has generally not been seen as characteristic of women offenders. However, I suggest it here as an area for further inquiry, especially within the context of the woman's total offending career.

Emphasis also should be placed on the role that physical community structures have in presenting criminal opportunities and sustaining women involved in crime. Of particular importance for Rochester's women were the bodegas, or corner stores, that have proliferated in the city's ghettos. Owners not only purchased stolen merchandise from the women but also serviced their personal needs by what they sold. The same was true of pawn shops, off-track betting parlors, bars, laundries, and virtually every establishment where people gathered. All meant customers or connections for the women's criminal activity, and all had some role in meeting their daily needs, whether for a bathroom, food, or just a place to rest.

Implied in the preceding discussions is the additional need for future research to approach crime and criminality not as a static entity but as something that changes over time because of both the skills of the person and the availability of criminal opportunity structures in the environment where the crime takes place. Thus, attention must be placed on the temporal dimension of the person's career for its impact on resourcefulness and skills, especially with respect to drug use, and the world of criminal opportunities in which the person operates.

Rochester's street women did not appear to begin in crime as agency-less victims of personal abuse, compelled to engage in prostitution or steal solely to obtain drugs as self-medication for past traumas. Instead, they expressed multiple motivations for becoming criminally involved, including status, the desire for fast money, the thrill they experienced when committing crime, or a family history with many and deep connections in the criminal world that provided both a learning environment and opportunities to practice crime. What the women subsequently did or became likewise was related not only to these past histories of abuse but also, and more so, to their own personal resources to access and navigate the criminal opportunity structures available to them.

Thus, as stated earlier, the women in this study were not one type of offender or another: They were not larcenists, prostitutes, or drug sellers. They did what they were able to do, sometimes successfully but many more times not, on the basis of where they were in their lives in terms of drug use and available opportunities. The time dimension, coupled with a recognition that these women were capable of agency and choice and not just solely drug driven, is thus critical to any future examination of low-level women offenders' criminal careers.

The place and role of drugs in criminal activity also should remain a focus of research. My study suggests that drugs should not be taken as a given, assumed cause or even as a constant, consuming presence in criminality. As I have discussed, for many of the women I studied drugs were not so much the cause of their crimes as they were the result of the lifestyles in which the women engaged after becoming criminally involved. Drugs not only intersected with family networks, the club scene, and living the fast life, but they also figured prominently, as I have discussed throughout this book, in the women's economic survival through crime, whether the women boosted stolen goods to dealers and their customers or copped drugs for a profit for partiers (see Denton & O'Malley, 2006). Moreover, the ingestion of drugs by these women was not something that was all-consuming at all points in their lives. Not only had the women in this study been in rehab "more times than [they] could count," but also many also exercised a great deal of choice and control over their use depending on the particular lick they were pursuing.

The victimization trajectory for female criminality not only negates the possibility of such choice and assumes the omnipresence of drugs in the crime picture but also deflects attention away from the influence of larger structural determinants on women's entry into and continued involvement in crime (see Maher et al., 2006). Thus, the issues of race and class and how they intersect with gender must remain a critical interest of future research.

Because of the focus and breadth of this study, it was not possible to scrutinize in any depth the interrelationships of race, class, and gender. However, I certainly saw what E. Miller (1986) initially highlighted in her work that prompted this study: There were, indeed, several racially distinct pathways into crime among the women. I did note some differences between my study and E. Miller's, though. For example, only one of my six groups resembled her street woman path most associated with African American women. Also, this path was not one in which domestic networks were distinct from deviant ones, as E. Miller found. Instead, it clearly reflected what Dunlap (1992) stated about the impact of the crack epidemic on the African American family and extended kin network: that addiction has undermined the traditional vital role played by African American women in keeping families intact and that kinship support systems have been overwhelmed by the "sheer numbers of children [who] must be cared for by the more stable households" (p. 203). Even more troubling, Dunlap implied, is the role now played by the wider kinship network in transmitting these behaviors:

> It is almost impossible for children growing up in these families to define themselves except in relation to the world of drugs that surrounds them. [What once rescued them from a drug orientation, the wider kin network], now only reinforces it and helps to isolate the individual further from mainstream' influences. (p. 204)

Research also suggests that the social construction of gender in African American and working class communities continues to change in response to the effects of concentrated poverty, the growing divestment of economic opportunities in the urban environment, and the removal of many community members from it, primarily young males, by the criminal justice system. Recall that only one of my groups, the Show Me the Money group, resembled the Baby Club discussed by Anderson (1999), and far more of the women in my study seemed quite male-like in terms of their adherence and demonstration of the toughness required by the code of their streets.

A final research interest of mine is the ultimate outcome(s) of these women or the whole issue of what becomes of low-level women offenders. When do they desist in crime, and why? Are the patterns found among male desisters also apparent for women, or does gender make a difference in terms of the availability of life chances as well as societal attitudes about it and crime? Maruna (2001) found few differences between men and women in the self-narratives that facilitated their desistance; however, his sample of only 10 women former offenders was extremely small. Much further research in this area is clearly warranted.

In conclusion, I must report that instead of finding Rochester's street women agencyless victims, failures, or damaged goods, I witnessed among them choice; rationality; and, more important, a great deal of resilience. I also found quite a few friends who shared much of their personal lives with me and even more of their time. Although I politely turned down near-daily invitations to lunch, I spent every Sunday afternoon with the women as they sat in their pajamas and argued over which movie to watch. I saw two babies born and participated in several women's baptismal celebrations, along with far too many birthdays.

I read and praised letters and crayoned pictures from the women's children and then sat and listened to how badly things had gone at those children's much-anticipated visits. I saw mothers sending notes to sons, housed elsewhere in the facility, and watched as older women looked after new arrivals who were daughters of street acquaintances or those who had just left. I welcomed back women who had been released hours or days earlier. I also heard many promises to myself and others, accompanied by just as many phone numbers, to stay in touch—most of which were broken.

I remain close to one of the women who is struggling financially, emotionally, and physically to maintain sobriety and stay away from the people, places, and things that would tempt her to do otherwise. She's living in an apartment (in essence, the second floor of a house) that consists of two rooms and a bath, with no stove, refrigerator, or kitchen sink. We see each other at least once a week, and she keeps me updated on several other women. Some she sees on the street, and a few she met during her most recent stay in jail for an assault. I also am aware of two who have died, both violently, in the past year: One was found in a lake and the other was killed during a police chase after she was observed boosting in a local mall. As this book ends and another begins, I probably will see more of my "new–old" friends on my next trip to jail. Although we will no doubt laugh and share good conversation as we reconnect, the pleasure will be bittersweet.

References

Adler, F. (1975). *Sisters in crime: The rise of the new female criminal.* New York: McGraw-Hill.

Agnew, R. (2006). *Pressured in crime.* Los Angeles: Roxbury.

Anderson, E. (1990). *Streetwise: Race, class, and change in an urban community.* Chicago: University of Chicago Press.

Anderson, E. (1999). *Code of the street: Decency, violence, and the moral life of the inner city.* New York: Norton.

Arnold, R. (1990). Processes of victimization and criminalization of Black women. *Social Justice, 17,* 153–166.

Bachman, R., & Schutt, R. (2003). *The practice of research in criminology and criminal justice.* Thousand Oaks, CA: Sage.

Bandura, A. (1986). *Social foundations of thought and action.* Englewood Cliffs, NJ: Prentice-Hall.

Bandura, A. (1997). *Self-efficacy: The exercise of control.* New York: W. H. Freeman.

Baskin, D., & Sommers, I. (1998). *Casualties of community disorder: Women's careers in violent crime.* Boulder, CO: Westview Press.

Baskin, D., Sommers, I., & Fagan, J. (1993). The political economy of female violent crime. *Fordham Urban Law Review, 20,* 401–407.

Becker, L. (1999, November 21). Rochester struggles with infant mortality. *Rochester Democrat and Chronicle.* Retrieved June 1, 2005, from http://libdb. sjfc.edu:3060/iw-search/we/InfoWeb

Belknap, J. (2007). *The invisible woman: Gender, crime, and justice.* Belmont, CA: Wadsworth/Thomas Learning.

Bourgois, P. (1989). In search of Horatio Alger: Culture and ideology in the crack economy. *Contemporary Drug Problems, 16,* 619–650.

Bourgois, P. (2003). *In search of respect: Selling crack in El Barrio* (2nd ed.). Cambridge, England: Cambridge University Press.

Bourgois, P., & Dunlap, E. (1993). Exorcising sex for crack: An ethnographic perspective from Harlem. In M. Ratner (Ed.), *Crack pipe as pimp: An ethnographic investigation of sex-for-crack exchanges* (pp. 97–132). New York: Lexington Books.

Bureau of Justice Statistics. (2005). *Prison and jail inmates at midyear 2004.* Washington, DC: U.S. Department of Justice.

Bureau of Justice Statistics. (2006a). *Medical problems of jail inmates.* Washington, DC: U.S. Department of Justice.

Bureau of Justice Statistics. (2006b). *Mental health problems of prison and jail inmates.* Washington, DC: U.S. Department of Justice.

Bureau of Justice Statistics. (2007). *Prison and jail inmates at midyear 2006.* Washington, DC: U.S. Department of Justice.

Centers for Disease Control and Prevention. (1999). High prevalence of chlamydian and gonococcal infection in women entering jails and juvenile detention centers—Chicago, Birmingham, and San Francisco, 1998. *Journal of the American Medical Association, 282,* 1417–1420.

Chesney-Lind, M., & Rodriguez, N. (1983). Women under lock and key: A view from the inside. *Prison Journal, 63,* 47–65.

Connell, R. W. (1987). *Gender & power.* Stanford, CA: Stanford University Press.

Cresswell, J. (1998). *Qualitative inquiry and research design: Choosing among five traditions.* Thousand Oaks, CA: Sage.

Dalla, R., Xia, Y., & Kennedy, H. (2003). "You just give them what they want and pray they don't kill you": Street-level sex workers' reports of victimization, personal resources, and coping strategies. *Violence Against Women, 9,* 1367–1394.

Daly, K. (1992). Women's pathways to felony court: Feminist theories and problems of representation. *Review of Law and Women's Studies, 2,* 11–51.

Danner, T., Blount, W., Silverman, I., & Vega, M. (1995). The female chronic offender: Exploring life contingency and offense history dimensions for incarcerated female offenders. *Women & Criminal Justice, 6*(2), 45–66.

DeLisi, M. (2002). Not just a boy's club: An empirical assessment of female career criminals. *Women & Criminal Justice, 13*(4), 27–45.

Denton, B., & O'Malley, P. (1999). Gender, trust, and business: Women drug dealers in the illicit economy. *British Journal of Criminology, 39,* 513–530.

Denton, B., & O'Malley, P. (2006). Property crime as it relates to women drug dealers. In L. F. Alarid & P. Cromwell (Eds.), *In her own words: Women offenders' views on crime and victimization* (pp. 203–212). Los Angeles: Roxbury.

Ditton, P. (1999). *Mental health and treatment of inmates and probationers* [Special report]. Washington, DC: U.S. Department of Justice, Bureau of Justice Statistics.

Droppleman, P., & Wilt, D. (1993). Women, depression, and anger. In S. Thomas (Ed.), *Women and anger* (pp. 209–232). New York: Springer Publishing Company.

Dunlap, E. (1992). Impact of drugs on family life and kin networks in the inner-city African American single-parent household. In A. Harrell & G. Peterson (Eds.), *Drugs, crime, and social isolation: Barriers to urban opportunity* (pp. 181–207). Washington, DC: Urban Institute Press.

Dunlap, E., & Johnson, B. (1996). Family and human resources in the development of a female crack-seller career: Case study of a hidden population. *Journal of Drug Issues, 26,* 175–199.

Emerson, R. (Ed.). (1983). *Contemporary field research: A collection of readings.* Boston: Little, Brown.

Emerson, R. (1988). *Contemporary field research.* Prospect Heights, IL: Waveland Press.

Erickson, P., Butters, J., McGillicuddy, P., & Hallgren, A. (2000). Crack and prostitution: Gender, myths, and experiences. *Journal of Drug Issues, 30,* 767–788.

Fagan, J. (1994). Women and drugs revisited: Female participation in the cocaine economy. *Journal of Drug Issues, 24,* 179–227.

Fleisher, M. (1995). *Beggars and thieves: Lives of urban street criminals.* Madison: University of Wisconsin Press.

Forgas, J., & Williams, K. (2002). *The social self.* New York: Psychology Press.

Freudenberg, N. (2002). Adverse effects of US jail and prison policies on the health and well-being of women of color. *American Journal of Public Health, 92,* 1895–1900.

Fullilove, M., & Lown, A. (1992). Crack 'hos and skeezers: Traumatic experiences of women crack users. *Journal of Sex Research, 29,* 275–288.

Gecas, V. (1989). The social psychology of self-efficacy. *American Sociological Review, 15,* 291–316.

Gellert, G., Maxwell, R., Higgins, K., Pendergast, T., & Wilker, N. (1993). HIV infection in the women's jail, Orange County, California, 1985 through 1991. *American Journal of Public Health, 83,* 1454–1456.

Gerling, C. (1957). *Smugtown, U.S.A.* Webster, NY: Plaza.

Giallombardo, R. (1966). *Society of women: A study of a women's prison.* New York: Wiley.

Gilfus, M. (1992). From victims to survivors to offenders: Women's routes of entry and immersion into street crime. *Women & Criminal Justice, 4*(1), 63–89.

Glaser, B., & Strauss, A. (1967). *The discovery of grounded theory.* New York: Aldine de Gruyter.

Goffman, E. (1959). *The presentation of self in everyday life.* New York: Anchor Books.

Goffman, E. (1963). *Stigma.* Englewood Cliffs, NJ: Prentice Hall.

Goldfarb, R. (1975). *Jails: The ultimate ghetto of the criminal justice system.* Garden City, NY: Anchor Books.

Goldstein, P., Ouellet, L., & Fendrich, M. (1992). From bag brides to skeezers: A historical perspective on sex for drugs behavior. *Journal of Psychoactive Drugs, 24,* 349–361.

Gottfredson, M., & Hirschi, T. (1990). *A general theory of crime.* Stanford, CA: Stanford University Press.

Green, A., Day, S., & Ward, H. (2000). Crack cocaine and prostitution in London in the 1990s. *Sociology of Health & Illness, 22,* 27–39.

Hanson, B., Beschner, J., Walters, J., & Bovelle, E. (1985). *Life without heroin.* Lexington, MA: Lexington Books.

Harrison, P., & Beck, J. (2005). *Prison and jail inmates at midyear 2004.* Washington, DC: U.S. Department of Justice.

Haywood, T., Kravitz, H., Goldman, L., & Freeman, A. (2000). Characteristics of women in jail and treatment orientations. *Behavior Modification, 24,* 307–324.

Henriques, Z., & Manatu-Rupert, N. (2001). Living on the outside: African American women before, during, and after imprisonment. *Prison Journal, 81,* 6–19.

Holmes, M., Safyer, S., Bickell, N., Vermund, S., Hanff, P., & Phillips, R. (1993). Chlamydia cervical infection in jailed women. *American Journal of Public Health, 83,* 551–555.

Howard, J., & Hollander, J. (1997). *Gendered situations, gendered selves.* Thousand Oaks, CA: Sage.

Inciardi, J., Lockwood, D., & Pottieger, A. (1999). *Women and crack-cocaine.* New York: Macmillan.

Irwin, J. (1970). *The felon.* Englewood Cliffs, NJ: Prentice Hall.

Irwin, J. (1975). *The jail: Managing the underclass in American society.* Berkeley: University of California Press.

Jacobs, B. (1999). *Dealing crack.* Boston: Northeastern University Press.

Johnson, B., Golub, A., & Fagan, J. (1995). Careers in crack, drug use, drug distribution, and non-drug criminality. *Crime and Delinquency, 41,* 275–291.

Katz, J. (1988). *Seductions of crime.* New York: Basic Books.

Kelley, B., Loeber, R., Keenan, K., & DeLamatre, M. (1997, November). Developmental pathways in boys' disruptive and delinquent behavior. *Juvenile Justice Bulletin,* 1–20.

Klofas, J. (2003). Rochester census and school data for *Paynter v. NY,* 2003. Retrieved March 26, 2005, from http://www.rit.edu/~jmkgcj/research/Other Studies/School.pdf

Klofas, J. (2004). *General data presentation, 2001–2004* (Working papers, Rochester Strategic Approaches to Community Safety Initiative). Retrieved March 1, 2006, from http://www.rit.edu/~jmkgcj/research/SACS1/Index.htm

Kvale, S. (1996). *Interviews: An introduction to qualitative research interviewing.* Thousand Oaks, CA: Sage.

Lewis, O. (1966). *La vida.* New York: Random House.

Lick. (n.d.). In *Urban dictionary.* Retrieved June 1, 2007, from http://www.urban dictionary.com

Liebow, E. (1993). *Tell them who I am: The lives of homeless women.* New York: Penguin Books.

Lofland, J. (1969). *Deviance and identity.* Englewood Cliffs, NJ: Prentice-Hall.

Maeve, M. K. (2001). Waiting to be caught: The devolution of health for women newly released from jail. *Criminal Justice Review, 26,* 143–169.

Maher, L. (1992). Reconstructing the female criminal: Women and crack cocaine. *Review of Law and Women's Studies, 2,* 131–154.

Maher, L. (1996). Hidden in the light: Occupational norms among crack-using street-level sex workers. *Journal of Drug Issues, 26,* 143–175.

Maher, L. (1997). *Sexed work: Gender, race, and resistance in a Brooklyn drug market.* Oxford, England: Clarendon Press.

Maher, L., & Daly, K. (1996). Women in the street-level drug economy: Continuity or change? *Criminology, 34,* 465–491.

Maher, L., Dunlap, E., & Johnson, B. (2006). Black women's pathways to involvement in illicit drug sales. In L. F. Alarid & P. Cromwell (Eds.), *In her own words* (pp. 15–31). Los Angeles: Roxbury.

Maher, L., Dunlap, E., Johnson, B., & Hamid, A. (1996). Gender, power, and alternative living arrangements in the inner-city crack culture. *Journal of Research in Crime and Delinquency, 33,* 181–205.

Maruna, S. (2001). *Making good: How ex-convicts reform and rebuild their lives.* Washington, DC: American Psychological Association.

Matza, D. (1969). *Becoming deviant.* Englewood Cliffs, NJ: Prentice Hall.

Maxwell, S., & Maxwell, C. (2000). Examining the "criminal careers" of prostitutes within the nexus of drug use, drug selling, and other illicit activities. *Criminology, 38,* 787–810.

McClelland, G., Teplin, L., Abram, K., & Jacobs, N. (2002). HIV and AIDS risk behaviors among female detainees: Implications for public health policy. *American Journal of Public Health, 92,* 818–826.

McGuire, J. (2004). *Understanding psychology and crime.* New York: Open University Press.

Meares, R. (2000). *Intimacy & alienation.* London: Routledge.

Meichenbaum, D. (1977). *Cognitive behavior modification: An integrative approach.* New York: Plenum Press.

Messerschmidt, J. (1997). *Crime as structured action.* Thousand Oaks, CA: Sage.

Metropolitan Forum. (1996). *Falling behind: The community of Monroe at the Millennium.* Retrieved March 26, 2005, from http://www.rit.edu/-metforum/bluebook.html

Mieczkowski, T. (1994). The experiences of women who sell crack: Some descriptive data from the Detroit Crack Ethnography Project. *Journal of Drug Issues, 24,* 227–248.

Miller, E. (1986). *Street women.* Philadelphia: Temple University Press.

Miller, J. (2001). *One of the guys: Girls, guys, and gender.* New York: Oxford University Press.

Monto, M. (2004). Female prostitution, customers, and violence. *Violence Against Women, 10,* 160–188.

Morgan, P., & Joe, K. (1997). Uncharted terrain: Contexts of experience among women in the illicit drug economy. *Women & Criminal Justice, 8*(3), 85–109.

Norton-Hawk, M. (2004). A comparison of pimp- and non-pimp-controlled women. *Violence Against Women, 10,* 189–194.

Owen, B. (1998). *In the mix: Struggle and survival in a women's prison.* Albany: State University of New York Press.

Parenti, C. (1999). *Lockdown America.* New York: Verso Books.

Patton, M. (2002). *Qualitative research and evaluation methods.* Thousand Oaks, CA: Sage.

Piquero, A. (2000). Assessing the relationships between gender, chronicity, seriousness, and offense skewness in criminal offending. *Journal of Criminal Justice, 28,* 103–115.

Piquero, A., & Chung, H. (2001). On the relationships between gender, early onset, and the seriousness of offending. *Journal of Criminal Justice, 29,* 189–206.

Pollock, J. (1986). *Sex and supervision: Guarding male and female inmates.* New York: Greenwood Press.

Pollock, J. (2002). *Women, prison, and crime.* Belmont, CA: Wadsworth/Thomson Learning.

Pryor, D. (2003). *Rochester and Monroe County community profile: How well are we doing?* Rochester, NY: Center for Governmental Research.

Ratner, M. (Ed.). (1993). *Crack pipe as pimp: An ethnographic investigation of sex-for-crack exchanges.* New York: Lexington Books.

Reinharz, S. (1992). *Feminist methods in social research.* New York: Oxford University Press.

Ritchie, B. (1996). *Compelled to crime: The gender entrapment of battered Black women.* New York: Routledge.

Rockell, B. A. (2004). *Street-life and survival in jail: A case study of women doing county time* [Unpublished paper]. University at Albany, Albany, New York.

Romenesko, K., & Miller, E. (1989). The second step in double jeopardy: Appropriating the labor of female street hustlers. *Crime & Delinquency, 35,* 109–135.

Rosenbaum, M. (1981). *Women on heroin.* New Brunswick, NJ: Rutgers University Press.

Samenow, S. (2004). *Inside the criminal mind* (2nd ed.). New York: Crown.

Sampson, R., & Laub, J. (1993). *Crime in the making: Pathways and turning points through life.* Cambridge, MA: Harvard University Press.

Scheff, T. (1990). *Microsociology.* Chicago: University of Chicago Press.

Seabrook, E. (1993). Women's anger and substance abuse. In S. Thomas (Ed.), *Women and anger* (pp. 186–208). New York: Springer Publishing Company.

Sharpe, T. (2005). *Behind the eight ball.* New York: Haworth Press.

Simon, R. (1975). *Women and crime.* Lexington, MA: Lexington Books.

Simp. (n.d.). In *Urban dictionary.* Retrieved June 1, 2007, from http://www.urbandictionary.com

Sommers, I., Baskin, D., & Fagan, J. (1996). The structural relationship between drug use, drug dealing, and other income support activities among women drug sellers. *Journal of Drug Issues, 26,* 975–1006.

Sommers, I., Baskin, D., & Fagan, J. (2000). *Workin' hard for the money: The social and economic lives of women drug sellers.* Huntington, NY: NOVA Science Publishers.

Steffensmeier, D. (1983). Organization properties and sex-segregation in the underworld: Building a sociological theory of sex differences in crime. *Social Forces, 61,* 1010–1032.

Steffensmeier, D., & Terry, R. (1986). Institutional sexism in the underworld: A view from the inside. *Sociological Inquiry, 56,* 304–323.

Stephens, R. (1991). *The street addict role.* Albany: State University of New York Press.

Sterk, C. (1999). *Fast lives: Women who use crack cocaine.* Philadelphia: Temple University Press.

Strauss, A., & Corbin, J. (1998). *Basics of qualitative research: Techniques and procedures for developing grounded theory.* Thousand Oaks, CA: Sage.

Surratt, H., Inciardi, J., Kurtz, S., & Kiley, M. (2004). Sex work and drug use in a subculture of violence. *Crime & Delinquency, 50,* 43–60.

Suttles, G. (1968). *The social order of the slum.* Chicago: University of Chicago Press.

Taylor, S., & Bogdan, R. (1998). *Introduction to qualitative research methods.* New York: Wiley.

Tea, M. (Ed.). (2003). *Without a net: The female experience of growing up working class.* Emeryville, CA: Avalon.

Teplin, L. (1990). The prevalence of severe mental disorder among male urban jail detainees. *American Journal of Public Health, 80,* 663–669.

Terry, C. (2003). *The fellas: Overcoming prison and addiction.* Belmont, CA: Wadsworth.

Thomas, S. (Ed.). (1993). *Women and anger.* New York: Springer Publishing Company.

Thornberry, T., & Krohn, M. (2001). The development of delinquency: An interactional perspective. In S. White (Ed.), *Handbook of youth and justice* (pp. 177–193). New York: Plenum Press.

U.S. Census Bureau. (2004). *Monroe County and Rochester New York quick facts.* Retrieved March 26, 2005, from http://quickfacts.census.gov/qfd/states/36/36055.html

Williamson, C., & Cluse-Tolar, T. (2002). Pimp-controlled prostitution: Still an integral part of street life. *Violence Against Women, 8,* 1074–1092.

Wilson, W. (1997). *When work disappears: The world of the new urban poor.* New York: Knopf.

Wright, R., & Decker, S. (1994). *Burglars on the job.* Boston: Northeastern University Press.

Index

About the Author

Barbara A. Rockell, PhD, is an assistant professor of sociology at St. John Fisher College in Rochester, New York. She joined the faculty in 2003 after a lengthy and diverse career in the field of criminal justice. Starting in the area of child protective services, she subsequently served in positions at the New York State Commission of Correction and Division of Criminal Justice Services. In 1990, Dr. Rockell joined the Monroe County Sheriff's Office in Rochester, New York, where she acted as the Sheriff's staff inspector. Dr. Rockell began her graduate studies in criminal justice at the University at Albany in 1977 but interrupted them shortly thereafter to pursue a career path in the field. She was readmitted to the School of Criminal Justice in 2003, where she completed her doctorate. She is currently completing research for a volume concerning jail use and confinement.